The International Jewish Songbook

compiled edited and arranged by
Velvel Pasternak

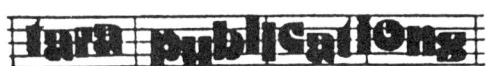

ISBN 0-933676-39-5

© 1994 by Tara Publications
All rights reserved. No part of this book
may be reproduced in any form without
permission in writing from the publisher

CONTENTS

SONGS OF ISRAEL
Ose Shalom /9
Am Yisraél Chai /10
Am Yisraél Chai II /10
Hévénu Shalom Aléchem /11
David Melech Yisraél /11
Chorshat Ha'ekaliptus /12
B'arvot Hanegev /14
Lu Y'hi /16
Ush'avtem Mayim/ 18
Dodi Li /19
Erets Yisraél Yafa /20
Artsa Alinu /22
Erev Ba /23
Hiné Ma Tov /24
Hiné Ma Tov II /25
Shiro Shel Aba /26
K'var Acharé Chatsot /27
Shir Hapalmach /28
Od Lo Ahavti Dai /30
Halicha L'késaria /31
Bashana Haba'a /32
Hava Nagila /34
O-le, O-le /35
Hafinjan /36
Erev Shel Shoshanim /37
T'fila /38
Zemer Atik /40
Tsena 41
Rad Halaila /42
Hakotel /44
El Ginat Egoz /46
Ma Avaréch /47
Al Kol Ele /48
Machar /50
Hamilchama Ha'achrona /52
Lach Y'rushalayim /54
Jerusalem of Gold-Y'-rushalayim Shel Zahav /56
Hal'luya /58
Chai /60
Nolad'ti L'shalom /62
Y'rushalayim /64
Sisu Et Y'rushalayim /66
Hatikva /68
Lo Yisa Goi /70

SONGS IN YIDDISH
Oifn Pripitchik /72
Rozhinkes Mit Mandlen /74
Der Rebe Elimelech /76
Eli Eli /78
Un Az Der Rebe Zingt /80
Bai Mir Bistu Shén /81
Eshes Chayil /84
A Yidishe Mame /85
Papirossen /88
Yankele /90
Di Grine Kuzine /92
M'chuténiste Maine /93
Tumbalalaika /94
A Brivele Der Mamen/ 96
Belz /98
Rézele /100
Yome Yome /101
Shén Vi Di L'vone /102
Vi Ahin Zol Ich Gén /104
S'brent /106
Zog Nit Kénmol /107
Shloimele Malkele /108
Zol Shoin Kumen Di G'ulo /110
Chiribim /112
Di M'zinke /114
Choson Kala Mazel Tov /115
Yossel, Yossel /116
Rumania, Rumania/ 118

SEPHARDIC & ORIENTAL
Cuando El Rey Nimrod /122
Los Bilbilicos /123
Scalerica D'oro /124
Yo M'enamori D'un Aire /126
Durme Durme /128
Hitragut /129
Ta'am Haman /130
Ocho Kandelikas /132
Lanér V'livsamim /133
Mizmor L'david /134
Mizmor L'david II /136
Yitsmach Shalom /138
Ets Harimon /139
Yom Ze L'yisraél /140
Ki Eshm'ra Shabat /141
Yigdal /142
D'ror Yikra /143
D'ror Yikra II /144
Ma'oz Tsur /145
Kadésh Ur'chats /146
Kadésh Ur'chats II /147

Quen Supiese /148
Az Yashir Moshe /149
Non Komo Muestro /150
Amen Shém Nora /151
Mipi El /152
Hamavdil /153

SONGS IN ENGLISH
Momele /156
Leaving Mother Russia /158
Jerusalem Is Mine /160
Dona, Dona /162
L'chi Lach /164
Light One Candle /167
My Zédi /168
Alef Bet /170

SABBATH & HOLIDAYS
Shabat Hamalka /172
Y'did Nefesh /173
L'cha Dodi /174
L'cha Dodi II /175
Adon Olam /176
Adon Olam II /178
Shabat Shalom /179
Shalom Alechem 180
Eshet Chayil 181
Ya Ribon /183
Tsur Mishelo /184
Shir Hama'alot /185
Shir Hama'alot II /186
Eliyahu Hanavi /187
Sisu V'simchu /188
Candle Blessings /189
Ma'oz Tsur /190
Mi Y'malél /191
S'vivon /192
Y'mé Hachanuka /193
Hine Ba /194
Chanuka Chag Yafe /195
I Have A Little Dreydl /196
Tu Bishvat /197
Ani Purim /198
Chag Purim /199
Ha Lachma Anya /200
Ma Nishtana /201
Ma Nishtana II /202
Avadim Hayinu /203

Dayénu /204
V'hi She'amda 205
Chad Gadya /206
Chad Gadya II /207
Adir Hu /208
Echad Mi Yodé'a /209
L'shana Haba'a /210
L'shana Haba'a II /210

CHASSIDIC & LITURGICAL
Y'varech'cha /212
Bilvavi /213
Tsiyon /214
Zara /215
Esa Enai /216
Moshe Emet /217
Ele Chamda Libi /218
Avinu Malkénu /219
Kol Ha'olam Kulo /220
V'haér Enénu /221
Shalom Rav /222
Ufaratsta /224
Sheyibane Bet Hamikdash /225
Yism'chu Hashamayim /226
Ki Mitsiyon /227
Ets Chayim Hi /228
Uva'u Ha'ovdim /230
Siman Tov /231
Od Yishama /232
Od Yishama II /233
Shehecheyanu /234
Birkat Hamazon /236
Mitsva G'dola /238
Ani Ma'amin /239
Eli Ata /240
Samchém /241
Mashiach /242
Nye Zu Ritse Chloptsi /244
Shmelkie's Nigun /245
Nigun /246
Nigun II /247
Nigun III /248
Nigun IV /248

SELECTED BIBLIOGRAPHY /249
INDEX OF FIRST LINES /250
SELECTED DISCOGRAPHY /252
ALPHABETICAL INDEX /254

ACKNOWLEDGMENTS

Grateful appreciation is extended to: my colleague, Seymour Silbermintz, noted musician, for his painstaking proofreading of this manuscript and for the suggestions, both musical and textual which have become a valuable part of this collection. Azriel Cohen, a member of our family and a fine graphic artist, for the cover art and illustrations. To my son, Gedalia, who was always available to assist with his technical expertise. My daughter, Shira Be'eri, for her valuable suggestions. To all the American artists who have graciously given permission for use of their recordings which appear in the accompanying cassette and compact disk. ACUM Ltd., for the reprint rights to the Israeli selections. Last but not least, to Goldie, my life-long partner, who once again willingly and graciously afforded me the time and space to prepare a large publication in the field of Jewish music.

FOREWORD

This collection, by no means exhaustive, has been conceived as an overview of popular Jewish songs of the 20th century. The six categories presented here will provide the Jewish music lover with a broad panorama of material heretofore unavailable in a single edition. Wherever possible, all verses to a song have been given, but space limitations have made this unfeasible in many cases. The "Selected Bibliography" in the back section will be helpful in finding editions which contain additional verses to many of these songs. The 23 selections which make up the accompanying cassette and CD Sampler are meant merely to give a taste of the songs found in the six sections. Translations, with the exception of the liturgical texts, are often in capsule form rather than word for word. This is due to the nature of the copyright laws with regard to some of the material. A functional transliteration scheme has been used and it is consistent with that employed in other Tara publications. Every effort has been made to clear and give proper credit to the copyright holders. In a number of cases copyright search has proved fruitless.

SONGS

OF
ISRAEL

KEY TO TRANSLITERATION

a	as in c*a*r
ai	as in s*i*gh
e	as in f*e*d
e	as in th*ey*
i	as in p*i*n or m*e*
o	as in f*o*rm or b*o*at
u	as in tr*u*e
'	as in *i*t
ch	as in Ba*ch*

OSE SHALOM

Music: N. Hirsh   Lyrics: Liturgy

Israel has been through a series of wars since its establishment as a state. From 1948 on, many of the country's popular songs have dealt with the theme of *shalom*, peace. This song with text from the prayer book, was introduced at the first Hassidic Song Festival in the Fall of 1969. It became one of Israel's most popular songs and rapidly spread to many Jewish communities throughout the world.

Allegro moderato

O-se sha-lom bim-ro-mav hu ya-a-se sha-lom a-lé-nu v'-al kol Yis-ra-él v'-im-ru im-ru A-men ya-a-se sha-lom ya-a-se sha-lom sha-lom a-lé-nu v'-al kol Yis-ra-él al kol Yis-ra-él

Fine

D.S. al Fine

ya-a-se sha-lom ya-a-se sha-lom sha-lom a-lé-nu v'-al kol Yis-ra-él

©by the Author. All rights reserved

O-se sha-lom bim-ro-mav
Hu ya-a-se sha-lom a-lé-nu
V'-al kol Yis-ra-él v'-im-ru a-mén

עֹשֶׂה שָׁלוֹם בִּמְרוֹמָיו
הוּא יַעֲשֶׂה שָׁלוֹם עָלֵינוּ
וְעַל כָּל יִשְׂרָאֵל וְאִמְרוּ אָמֵן

May He who makes peace in the high places make peace for Israel and for all mankind and say Amen.

AM YISRAEL CHAI

S. Carlebach

This melody by Shlomo Carlebach became one of the theme songs used by the "Student Struggle For Soviet Jewry", an organization which lobbied throughout the world for the release of Jews in Russia.

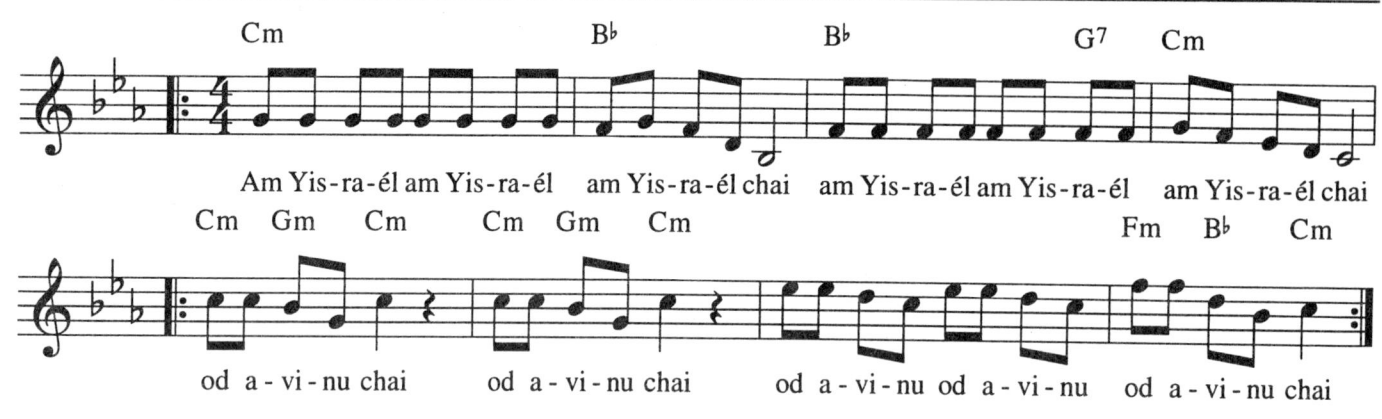

AM YISRAEL CHAI II

S. Rockoff

Am Yis-ra-él chai
Od A-vi-nu Chai

The Jewish people lives! Our Father yet lives!

עַם יִשְׂרָאֵל חַי
עוֹד אָבִינוּ חַי

HÉVÉNU SHALOM ALÉCHEM

Hé-vé-nu sha-lom a-lé-chem

הֲבֵאנוּ שָׁלוֹם עֲלֵיכֶם

Peace be unto you.

DAVID MELECH YISRAEL

Da-vid me-lech Yis-ra-él chai v'ka-yam

דָּוִד מֶלֶךְ יִשְׂרָאֵל חַי וְקַיָּם

David, King of Israel lives forever!

CHORSHAT HA'EKALIPTUS

N. Shemer

K'-she-i-ma ba-a hé-na ya-fa u-ts'-i-ra	כְּשֶׁאִמָּא בָּאָה הֵנָה יָפָה וּצְעִירָה
Az a-ba al giv-a ba-na la ba-yit	אָז אַבָּא עַל גִּבְעָה בָּנָה לָהּ בַּיִת
Chal-fu ha-a-vi-vim cha-tsi mé-a av-ra	חָלְפוּ הָאֲבִיבִים חֲצִי מֵאָה עָבְרָה
V'-tal-ta-lim haf-chu sé-va bén-ta-yim	וְתַלְתַּלִים הָפְכוּ שֵׂיבָה בֵּינְתַיִם
Refrain	פִּזְמוֹן
A-val al chof yar-dén	אֲבָל עַל חוֹף יַרְדֵּן
K'-mo m'-u-ma lo ka-ra	כְּמוֹ מְאוּמָה לֹא קָרָה
O-ta ha-du-mi-ya	אוֹתָהּ הַדּוּמִיָּה
V'-gam o-ta ha-taf-u-ra	וְגַם אוֹתָהּ הַתַּפְאוּרָה
Chor-shat ha-e-ka-lip-tus	חוֹרְשַׁת הָאֶקָלִיפְּטוּס
Ha-ge-sher ha-si-ra	הַגֶּשֶׁר הַסִּירָה
V'-ré-ach ha-ma-lu-ach	וְרֵיחַ הַמָּלוּחַ
Al ha-ma-yim	עַל הַמַּיִם
Mé-é-ver la-yar-dén ra-a-mu ha-to-ta-chim	מֵעֵבֶר לַיַּרְדֵּן רָעֲמוּ הַתּוֹתָחִים
V'-ha-sha-lom cha-zar b'-sof ha-ka-yitz	וְהַשָּׁלוֹם חָזַר בְּסוֹף הַקַּיִץ
V'-chol ha-ti-no-kot ha-yu la-a-na-shim	וְכָל הַתִּינוֹקוֹת הָיוּ לָאֲנָשִׁים
V'-shuv al ha-giv-a hé-ki-mu ba-yit (Refrain)	וְשׁוּב עַל הַגִּבְעָה הֵקִימוּ בַּיִת (פִּזְמוֹן)

The grove of Eucalyptus, the bridge, the wooden boat and the scent of mint floating above the water—all these have remained the same as if untouched by the passing of time.

B'ARVOT HANEGEV

Music: M. Baharav   Lyrics: R. Klatchkin

This moving song, Russian in flavor, was one of the favorite songs of the pioneers in the new State of Israel. An English version titled "The Little Bird is Calling" achieved a degree of popularity.

©Edition Negen, ACUM Israel

B'-ar-vot ha-ne-gev mit-no-tséts ha-tal	בְּעַרְבוֹת הַנֶּגֶב מִתְנוֹצֵץ הַטַל
B'-ar-vot ha-ne-gev ish ma-gén na-fal	בְּעַרְבוֹת הַנֶּגֶב אִישׁ מָגֵן נָפַל
Lo no-shém ha-na-ar v'-na-dam ha-lév	לֹא נוֹשֵׁם הַנַעַר וְנָדַם הַלֵב
Et b'-lo-rit ha-sa-ar ru-ach t'-latéf	אֶת בְּלוֹרִית הַשַׂעַר רוּחַ תְּלַטֵף
Ha-lu-mat a-tse-vet v'-ya-gon no-ra	הֲלוּמַת עֲצֶבֶת וְיָגוֹן נוֹרָא
Ém z'-ké-na ni-tse-vet v'-no-sét d'-va-ra	אֵם זְקֵנָה נִצֶבֶת וְנוֹשֵׂאת דְבָרָה
Ha-dim-a ni-ge-ret mé-é-né im-cha	הַדִמְעָה נִגֶרֶת מֵעֵינֵי אִמְךָ
Ba ka-dur o-fe-ret va-yif-lach lib-cha	בָּא כַּדוּר עוֹפֶרֶת וַיִפְלַח לִבְּךָ
Et b'-cho-ri sha-chal-ti bim-tsu-lot ha-yam	אֶת בְּכוֹרִי שָׁכַלְתִי בִּמְצוּלוֹת הַיָם
V'-ot-cha gi-dal-ti l'-ma-gén ha-am	וְאוֹתְךָ גִדַלְתִי לְמָגֵן הָעָם
Hém lo yish-b'-ru-nu b'-yat-mut u-sh'-chol	הֵם לֹא יִשְׁבְּרוּנוּ בְּיַתְמוּת וּשְׁכוֹל
Hém lo ya-ak-ru-nu, b'-ni lam-rot ha-kol	הֵם לֹא יַעַקְרוּנוּ בְּנִי לַמְרוֹת הַכֹּל
Az tsa-ad ka-di-ma na-ar g'-va ko-ma	אָז צָעַד קָדִימָה נַעַר גְבַהּ קוֹמָה
Va-yo-mar la ima al lach b'-dim-a	וַיֹאמַר לָהּ אִמָא אַל לָךְ בְּדִמְעָה
Ba-chu-ré-nu i-ma bi-mé p'-ku-da	בַּחוּרֵינוּ אִמָא בִּימֵי פְּקוּדָה
Mul son-é-nu i-ma k'-cho-mat p'-la-da	מוּל שׂוֹנְאֵינוּ אִמָא כְּחוֹמַת פְּלָדָה
Mul sho-déd va-me-lech ts'-mé da-mim ev-yon	מוּל שׁוֹדֵד וָמֶלֶךְ צְמֵא דָמִים אֶבְיוֹן
T'-ni-ni v'-e-he-ye lach a-no-chi l'-vén	תְנִינִי וְאֶהְיֶה לָךְ אָנֹכִי לְבֵן
B'-ar-vot ha-ne-gev hu la-chats ya-da	בְּעַרְבוֹת הַנֶּגֶב הוּא לָחַץ יָדָהּ
Im tir-tsu chev-ra-ya én zo a-ga-da	אִם תִרְצוּ חֶבְרַיָא אֵין זוֹ אַגָדָה

A boy has fallen in the Negev. As his mother mourns her loss, a tall youth steps forward and offers himself as her son. In the desolate Negev he grasps her hand. "If you will it, friends, it is no legend."

LU Y'HI

N. Shemer

©by the Author. All rights reserved

Od yésh mif-ras la-van ba-o-fek	עוֹד יֵשׁ מִפְרָשׂ לָבָן בָּאוֹפֶק
Mul a-nan sha-chor ka-véd	מוּל עָנָן שָׁחוֹר כָּבֵד
Kol she-n'-va-késh lu y'-hi	כָּל שֶׁנְּבַקֵּשׁ לוּ יְהִי
V'-im ba-cha-lo-not ha-e-rev	וְאִם בַּחֲלוֹנוֹת הָעֶרֶב
Or né-rot ha-chag ro-éd	אוֹר נֵרוֹת הַחַג רוֹעֵד
Kol she-n'-va-késh lu y'-hi	כָּל שֶׁנְּבַקֵּשׁ לוּ יְהִי.
Refrain	פזמון
Lu y'-hi a-na lu y'hi	לוּ יְהִי לוּ יְהִי אָנָא לוּ יְהִי
Kol she-n'-va-késh lu y'hi	כָּל שֶׁנְּבַקֵּשׁ לוּ יְהִי
Ma kol a-not a-ni sho-mé-a	מַה קוֹל עֲנוֹת אֲנִי שׁוֹמֵעַ
Kol sho-far v'-kol tu-pim	קוֹל שׁוֹפָר וְקוֹל תֻּפִּים
Kol she-n'-va-késh lu y'-hi	כָּל שֶׁנְּבַקֵּשׁ לוּ יְהִי
Lu ti-sha-ma b'-toch kol é-le	לוּ תִּשָּׁמַע בְּתוֹךְ כָּל אֵלֶה
Gam t'-fi-la a-chat mi-pi	גַּם תְּפִלָּה אַחַת מִפִּי
Kol she-n'-va-késh lu y'-hi *Refrain*	כָּל שֶׁנְּבַקֵּשׁ לוּ יְהִי פזמון
B'-toch sh'-chu-na k'-ta-na mu-tse-let	בְּתוֹךְ שְׁכוּנָה קְטַנָּה מֻצֶּלֶת
Ba-yit kat im gag a-dom	בַּיִת קָט עִם גַּג אָדֹם
Kol she-n'-va-késh lu y'-hi	כָּל שֶׁנְּבַקֵּשׁ לוּ יְהִי
Ze sof ha-ka-yits sof ha-de-rech	זֶה סוֹף הַקַּיִץ סוֹף הַדֶּרֶךְ
Tén la-hem la-shuv ha-lom	תֵּן לָהֶם לָשׁוּב הֲלוֹם
Kol she-n'-va-késh lu y'-hi *Refrain*	כָּל שֶׁנְּבַקֵּשׁ לוּ יְהִי פזמון
V'-im pit-om yiz-rach mé-o-fel	וְאִם פִּתְאוֹם יִזְרַח מֵאֹפֶל
Al ro-shé-nu or ko-chav	עַל רֹאשֵׁנוּ אוֹר כּוֹכָב
Kol she-n'-va-késh lu y'-hi	כָּל שֶׁנְּבַקֵּשׁ לוּ יְהִי
Az tén shal-va v'-tén gam ko-ach	אָז תֵּן שַׁלְוָה וְתֵן גַּם כֹּחַ
L'-chol é-le she-no-hav	לְכָל אֵלֶה שֶׁנֹּאהַב
Kol she-n'-va-késh lu y'-hi *Refrain*	כָּל שֶׁנְּבַקֵּשׁ לוּ יְהִי פזמון

A white sail facing a black cloud can be seen in the distance and through the distance the festive lights shimmer. All that we ask is "let it be."

USH'AVTEM MAYIM

Music: E. Amiran   Lyrics: Isaiah 12: 3

One of the best known circle dances of Israel. With text based on Isaiah, this dance is performed throughout the Jewish world.

Ush-av-tem ma-yim b'sa-son
Mi-mai-né ha-y'-shu-a

וּשְׁאַבְתֶּם מַיִם בְּשָׂשׂוֹן
מִמַּעַיְנֵי הַיְשׁוּעָה

Joyfully shall you draw from the fountains of deliverance.

DODI LI

Music: N. Chen Lyrics: Song of Songs

Although the authorship of this song is known, the melody has already assumed the status of a folk song. It is often used as a processional for the Jewish wedding ceremony and is also a well known folk dance.

©by the Author. All rights reserved

Refrain
Do-di lo va-a-ni lo ha-ro-e ba-sho-sha-nim

Mi zot o-la min ha-mid-bar
Mi zot o-la
M'-ku-te-ret mor u-l'vo-na   *Refrain*

Li-bav-ti-ni a-cho-ti ka-la
Li-bav-ti-ni ka-la   *Refrain*

U-ri tsa-fon u-vo-i té-man   *Refrain*

פזמון
דּוֹדִי לִי וַאֲנִי לוֹ הָרוֹעֶה בַּשּׁוֹשַׁנִּים

מִי זֹאת עוֹלָה מִן הַמִּדְבָּר
מִי זֹאת עוֹלָה
מְקֻטֶּרֶת מוֹר וּלְבוֹנָה (פזמון)

לִבַּבְתִּינִי אֲחוֹתִי כַּלָּה
לִבַּבְתִּינִי כַּלָּה (פזמון)

עוּרִי צָפוֹן וּבוֹאִי תֵימָן (פזמון)

My beloved is mine and I am his that feedeth among the lilies.

ERETS YISRAEL YAFA

Music: Y. Paikov Lyrics: D. Barak

Na-a-ra to-va y'-fat é-na-yim	נַעֲרָה טוֹבָה יְפַת עֵינַיִם
La-nu yésh b'-e-rets Yis-ra-él	לָנוּ יֵשׁ בְּאֶרֶץ יִשְׂרָאֵל
V'-ye-led tov Y'-ru-sha-la-yim	וְ"יֶלֶד טוֹב יְרוּשָׁלַיִם"
Ho mi pi-lél u-mi mi-lél	הוֹ מִי פִלֵל וּמִי מִלֵל
V'-to-ra o-ra ka-zo yésh la-nu	וְתוֹרָה אוֹרָה כָּזוֹ יֵשׁ לָנוּ
V'-gam ha-ga-da u-m'-gi-la	וְגַם הַגָדָה וּמְגִלָה
V'-e-lo-him e-chad she-la-nu	וֵאלֹהִים אֶחָד שֶׁלָנוּ
V'-kol cha-tan v'-kol ka-la	וְקוֹל חָתָן וְקוֹל כַּלָה
Refrain	פזמון
E-rets Yisrael ya-fa	אֶרֶץ יִשְׂרָאֵל יָפָה
E-rets Yis-ra-él po-ra-chat	אֶרֶץ יִשְׂרָאֵל פּוֹרַחַת
At yosh-va ba v'-tso-fa	אַתְּ יוֹשְׁבָה בָּה וְצוֹפָה
At tso-fa ba v'-zo-ra-chat	אַתְּ צוֹפָה בָּה וְזוֹרַחַת

Beautiful Land of Israel, flowering Land of Israel. You dwell there and look forth, you look forth and shine.

ARTSA ALINU

Folktune

An early pioneer song of unknown authorship, *Artsa Alinu* became one of the most popular vehicles for the "Hora", Israel's national dance. The song proclaims that although we have returned to our homeland and have begun our work, the fruit of our labors is yet to come.

Ar-tsa a-li-nu
K'var cha-rash-nu v'-gam za-ra-nu
A-val od lo ka-tsar-nu

אַרְצָה עָלִינוּ
כְּבָר חָרַשְׁנוּ וְגַם זָרַעְנוּ
אֲבָל עוֹד לֹא קָצַרְנוּ

We have come to our beloved land. We have plowed and planted but we have not yet harvested our crop.

EREV BA

Music: A. Levanon   Lyrics: O. Avissar

One of the early Israel Song Festivals produced this song. It has become a favorite throughout the world and is often used as a processional during the Jewish wedding ceremony.

©Edition Negen, ACUM Israel

Shuv ha-é-der no-hér bim-vo-ot hak-far
V'-o-le ha-a-vak mish-vi-lé a-far
V'-har-chék od tse-med in-ba-lim
M'-la-ve et me-shech hats-la-lim
E-rev ba
Shuv ha-ru-ach lo-chésh bén gid-rot ga-nim
Uv-tsa-me-ret ha-brosh k'-var na-mot yo-nim
V'har-chék al ke-tef hag-va-ot
Od nosh-kot kar-na-yim ach-ro-not
Erev ba
Shuv ha-ve-red cho-lém cha-lo-mot ba-lat
U-for-chim ko-cha-vim ba-ma-rom at at
V'-har-chék ba-é-mek ha-a-fél
M'-la-ve ha-tan et bo ha-lél
La-yil rad

שׁוּב הָעֵדֶר נוֹהֵר בִּמְבוֹאוֹת הַכְּפָר
וְעוֹלֶה הָאָבָק מִשְׁבִילֵי עָפָר
וְהַרְחֵק עוֹד צֶמֶד עֲנָבָלִים
מְלַוֶּה אֶת מֶשֶׁךְ הַצְּלָלִים
עֶרֶב בָּא
שׁוּב הָרוּחַ לוֹחֵשׁ בֵּין גְּדֵרוֹת גַּנִּים
וּבְצַמֶּרֶת הַבְּרוֹשׁ כְּבָר נָמוֹת יוֹנִים
וְהַרְחֵק עַל כֶּתֶף הַגְּבָעוֹת
עוֹד נוֹשְׁקוֹת קַרְנַיִם אַחֲרוֹנוֹת
עֶרֶב בָּא
שׁוּב הַוֶּרֶד חוֹלֵם חֲלוֹמַת בַּלָּאט
וּפוֹרְחִים כּוֹכָבִים בַּמָּרוֹם אַט אַט
וְהַרְחֵק בָּעֵמֶק הָאָפֵל
מְלַוֶּה הַתַּן אֶת בּוֹא הַלֵּיל
לַיִל רַד

Again the flock is flowing to the outskirts of the city and the dust rises up from the paths. Far away the bells accompany the coming of the shadows. Evening comes, evening comes.

HINÉ MA TOV

Folktune adapted by Jacobson
Lyrics: Psalm 133:1

Hi-né ma tov u-ma na-im
She-vet a-chim gam ya-chad

הִנֵּה מַה טּוֹב וּמַה נָּעִים
שֶׁבֶת אַחִים גַּם יָחַד

Behold how good and pleasant it is for brothers to dwell in unity.

Folktune   Lyrics: Psalm 133: 1

SHIRO SHEL ABA

N. Shemer

Im ba-har cha-tsav-ta e-ven l'-ha-kim bin-yan cha-dash
Ba-har cha-tsav-ta e-ven l'-ha-kim bin-yan cha-dash
Lo la-shav a-chi cha-tsav-ta l'-vin-yan cha-dash
Ki min ha-a-va-nim ha-é-lu yi-ba-ne ha-mik-dash
Yi-ba-ne ha-mik-dash

אִם בָּהָר חָצַבְתָּ אֶבֶן לְהָקִים בִּנְיָן חָדָשׁ
בָּהָר חָצַבְתָּ אֶבֶן לְהָקִים בִּנְיָן חָדָשׁ
לֹא לַשָּׁוְא אָחִי חָצַבְתָּ לְבִנְיָן חָדָשׁ
כִּי מִן הָאֲבָנִים הָאֵלּוּ
יִבָּנֶה הַמִּקְדָּשׁ

If you have cleared stones upon the mountain to build a new home, then your work, my brother, has not been in vain. From just such work the Temple will be rebuilt.

K'VAR ACHARÉ CHATSOT

Music N. Hirsh Lyrics: A. Ettinger

© by the authors. All rights reserved

K'-var a-cha-ré cha-tsot od lo ki-bu et ha-ya-ré-ach
Ki lif-né ki-bu o-rot, orot shel ko-cha-vim
Not-nim od re-ga kat la-o-ha-vim
Ma-char yi-ye ze yom cha-dash u-ma ef-shar
Mi-yom cha-dash k'-var l'-tsa-pot
Az tén la-nu od re-ga rak od re-ga
Af al pi she-k'-var ach-ré chatsot

כְּבָר אַחֲרֵי חֲצוֹת עוֹד לֹא כָּבוּ אֶת הַיָּרֵחַ
כִּי לִפְנֵי כְּבוּי אוֹרוֹת, אוֹרוֹת שֶׁל כּוֹכָבִים
נוֹתְנִים עוֹד רֶגַע קָט לָאוֹהֲבִים
מָחָר יִהְיֶה זֶה יוֹם חָדָשׁ וּמַה אֶפְשָׁר
מִיּוֹם חָדָשׁ כְּבָר לְצַפּוֹת
אָז תֵּן לָנוּ עוֹד רֶגַע רַק עוֹד רֶגַע
אַף עַל פִּי שֶׁכְּבָר אַחֲרֵי חֲצוֹת

Midnight has passed. Before the stars fade grant another moment to those in love.

SHIR HAPALMACH

SHIR HAPALMACH has been the official marching song of the I.D.F. (Israel Defense Forces), the successor to the original *Palmach*.

Music: D. Zahavi   Lyrics: Z. Gilead

©Tarbut Vechinuch Ed., ACUM Israel

Mi-sa-viv yé-hom ha-sa-ar	מִסָּבִיב יֵהוֹם הַסַּעַר
Ach ro-shé-nu lo yi-shach	אַךְ רֹאשֵׁנוּ לֹא יִשַּׁח
Lif-ku-da ta-mid a-nach-nu ta-mid	לִפְקוּדָה תָּמִיד אֲנַחְנוּ תָּמִיד
A-nu Ha-pal-mach	אָנוּ הַפַּלְמָ"ח
Mi-m'-tu-la ad ha-ne-gev	מִמְּטוּלָה עַד הַנֶּגֶב
Min ha-yam ad ha-mid-bar	מִן הַיָּם עַד הַמִּדְבָּר
Kol ba-chur v'-tov la-ne-shek	כָּל בָּחוּר וְטוֹב לַנֶּשֶׁק
Kol ba-chur al ha-mish-mar	כָּל בָּחוּר עַל הַמִּשְׁמָר
N'-tiv la-ne-sher ba-sha-ma-yim	נְתִיב לַנֶּשֶׁר בַּשָּׁמַיִם
Sh'-vil la-pe-re bén ha-rim	שְׁבִיל לַפֶּרֶא בֵּין הָרִים
Mul o-yév dar-ké-nu ya-al	מוּל אוֹיֵב דַּרְכֵּנוּ יַעַל
Bén nik-rot u-vén tsu-rim	בֵּין נְקָרוֹת וּבֵין צוּרִים
Ri-sho-nim ta-mid a-nach-nu	רִאשׁוֹנִים תָּמִיד אֲנַחְנוּ
L'-or ha-yom u-va-mach-shach	לְאוֹר הַיּוֹם וּבַמַּחְשָׁךְ
Lif-ku-da ta-mid a-nach-nu ta-mid	לִפְקוּדָה תָּמִיד אֲנַחְנוּ תָּמִיד
A-nu Ha-pal-mach	אָנוּ הַפַּלְמָ"ח

The storm rages around us but our heads are unbowed. We are always prepared—we are the Palmach. From Metulah to the Negev, from the sea to the desert, every man is combat ready: every man is on guard. We are the Palmach.

OD LO AHAVTI DAI

N. Shemer

B'-é-le ha-ya-da-yim od lo ba-ni-ti kfar
Od lo ma-tsa-ti ma-yim b'-em-tsa ha-mid-bar
Od lo tsi-ar-ti pe-rach od lo gi-li-ti éch
To-vil o-ti ha-de-rech ul'-an a-ni ho-léch
A-ai od lo a-hav-ti dai
Ha-ru-ach v'-ha-she-mesh al pa-nai
A-ai od lo a-mar-ti dai
V'-im lo ach-shav é-ma-tai

בְּאֵלֶה הַיָּדַיִם עוֹד לֹא בָּנִיתִי כְּפָר
עוֹד לֹא מָצָאתִי מַיִם בְּאֶמְצַע הַמִּדְבָּר
עוֹד לֹא צָרַתִי פֶּרַח עוֹד לֹא גִּילִיתִי אֵיךְ
תּוֹבִיל אוֹתִי הַדֶּרֶךְ וּלְאָן אֲנִי הוֹלֵךְ
אַי־עוֹד לֹא אָהַבְתִּי דַי
הָרוּחַ וְהַשֶּׁמֶשׁ עַל פָּנַי
אַי־עוֹד לֹא אָמַרְתִּי דַי
וְאִם לֹא עַכְשָׁיו אֵימָתַי

With these hands I have not yet rebuilt my homeland. There is so much that I have not yet accomplished and If I do not do it now—when?

HALICHA L'KÉSARIA

Music: D. Zehavi   Lyrics: H. Senesh

Born in Hungary, Hannah Senesh emigrated to Israel at age eighteen. During World War II, she volunteered for a secret mission with the British Air Force and parachuted into Yugoslavia to make contact with the Resistant forces and to help rescue Jews.

©Tarbut Vechinuch Ed., ACUM Israel

É-li she-lo yi-ga-mér l'-o-lam
Ha-chol v'-ha-yam
Rish-rush shel ha-ma-yim
B'-rak ha-sha-ma-yim
T'fi-lat ha-a-dam

אֵלִי שֶׁלֹא יִגָּמֵר לְעוֹלָם
הַחוֹל וְהַיָּם
רִשְׁרוּשׁ שֶׁל הַמַּיִם
בְּרַק הַשָּׁמַיִם
תְּפִלַּת הָאָדָם

My God...never end the sand and the sea, the ocean's roar, the sparkling skies, the prayer of man.

BASHANA HABA'A

Music: N. Hirsh   Lyrics: E. Manor

Since this song was first heard in 1969, it has become an international favorite. Versions have appeared in many languages. *Bashana's* popularity was increased by its use as the background for a series of American television commercials for the El Al airline and the Israel Ministry of Tourism.

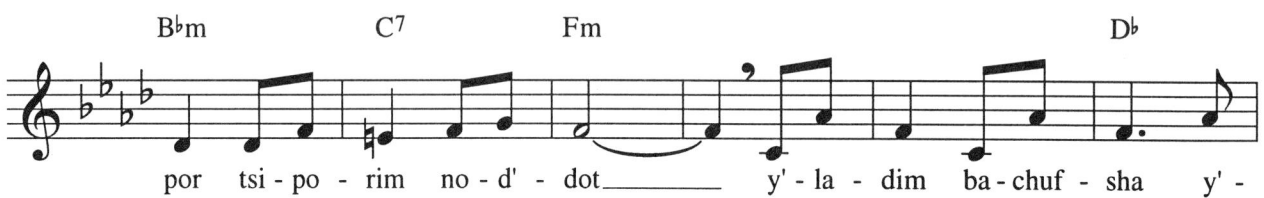

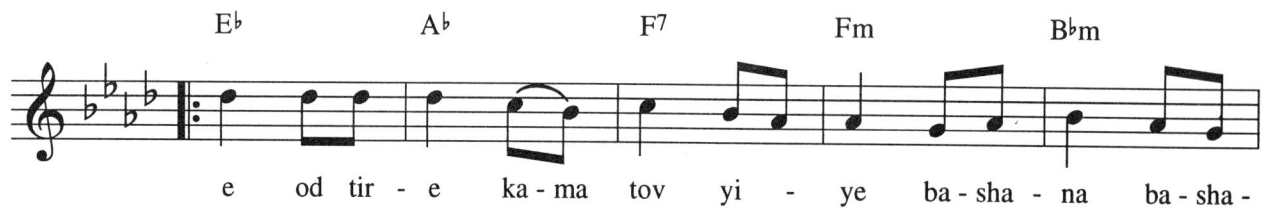
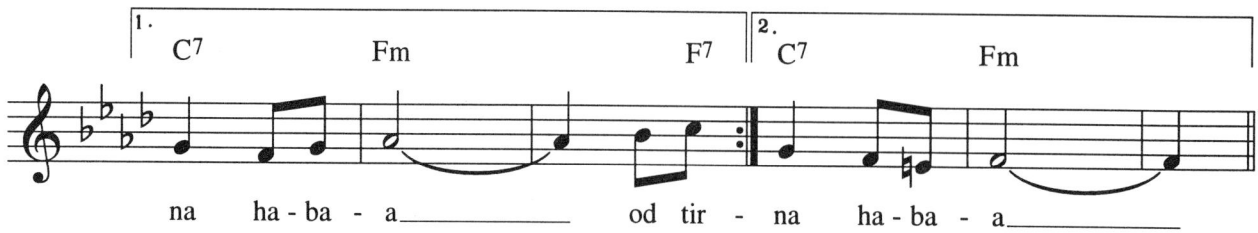

©by the Author. All rights reserved

Ba-sha-na ha-ba-a né-shév al ha-mir-pe-set	בַּשָּׁנָה הַבָּאָה נֵשֵׁב עַל הַמִרְפֶּסֶת
V'-nis-por tsi-po-rim no-d'-dot	וְנִסְפֹּר צִפֳּרִים נוֹדְדוֹת
Y'-la-dim ba-chuf-sha y'-sa-cha-ku to-fe-set	יְלָדִים בַּחֻפְשָׁה יְשַׂחֲקוּ תּוֹפֶסֶת
Bén ha-ba-yit l'-vén ha-sa-dot	בֵּין הַבַּיִת לְבֵין הַשָּׂדוֹת
Refrain	פזמון
Od tir-e, od tir-e	עוֹד תִּרְאֶה עוֹד תִּרְאֶה
Ka-ma tov yi-ye	כַּמָה טוֹב יִהְיֶה
Ba-sha-na ha-ba-a	בַּשָּׁנָה הַבָּאָה
A-na-vim a-du-mim yav-shi-lu ad ha-e-rev	עֲנָבִים אֲדוּמִים יַבְשִׁילוּ עַד הָעֶרֶב
V'-yug-shu tso-n'-nim la-shul-chan	וְיוּגְּשׁוּ צוֹנְנִים לַשֻּׁלְחָן
V'-ru-chot r'-du-mim yis-u el ém ha-de-rech	וְרוּחוֹת רְדוּמִים יִשְׂאוּ אֶל אֵם הַדֶּרֶךְ
I-to-nim y'-sha-nim v'-a-nan *Refrain*	עִתּוֹנִים יְשָׁנִים וְעָנָן פזמון
Ba-sha-na ha-ba-a nif-ros ka-pot ya-da-yim	בַּשָּׁנָה הַבָּאָה נִפְרֹשׂ כַּפּוֹת יָדַיִם
Mul ha-or ha-ni-gar ha-la-van	מוּל הָאוֹר הַנִּגָּר הַלָּבָן
A-na-fa l'-va-na tif-ros ba-or k'-na-fa-yim	אֲנָפָה לְבָנָה תִּפְרֹשׂ בָּאוֹר כְּנָפַיִם
V'-ha-she-mesh tiz-rach b'-to-chan *Refrain*	וְהַשֶּׁמֶשׁ תִּזְרַח בְּתוֹכָן פזמון

Next year, when peace will come, we shall return to the simple pleasures of life so long denied us. You will see, you will see, O how good it will be next year!

O-LE O-LE

Music: K. Oshrat   Lyrics: B. Z. Hamotal

Or ut-ché-let ba-sha-ma-yim
V'-yo-réd l'-fe-ta yom
A-na-nim hof-chim l'-ma-yim
Ke-shet o-la ba-ma-rom
Sh'-lal g'-va-nim v'-or sha-ma-yim
Ha-tsov-im et ha-o-lam
V'-ya-fe hu shiv-a-ta-yim
U-m'-cha-yéch l'-chu-lam
O-le o-le ha-shir b'-ya-chad
K'-she-ha-sim-cha ba-lév po-ra-chat
O-le o-le na-shir v'-ya-chad
Ga-dol v'-ka-tan k'-mo ke-shet b'-a-nan

©Gogly Music, ACUM Israel

אוֹר וּתְכֵלֶת בַּשָּׁמַיִם
וְיוֹרֵד לְפֶתַע יוֹם
עֲנָנִים הוֹפְכִים לְמַיִם
קֶשֶׁת עוֹלָה בַּמָּרוֹם
שְׁלַל גְּוָנִים וְאוֹר שָׁמַיִם
הַצּוֹבְעִים אֶת הָעוֹלָם
וְיָפֶה הוּא שִׁבְעָתַיִים
וּמְחַיֵּךְ לְכוּלָם
עוֹלֶה עוֹלֶה הַשִּׁיר בְּיַחַד
כְּשֶׁהַשִּׂמְחָה בַּלֵּב פּוֹרַחַת
עוֹלֶה עוֹלֶה הַשִּׁיר וְיַחַד
גָּדוֹל וְקָטָן כְּמוֹ קֶשֶׁת בֶּעָנָן

Light and blue in the heavens and suddenly day descends. Clouds turn to water and rainbow rises in the sky. The world is colored by brilliant hues and heavenly light. Arise, arise and sing together.

HAFINJAN

Music: Folktune   Lyrics: C. Hefer

The word "finjan" is Arabic and means coffee pot. This song with its lovely lilt and interspersed hand claps has become a favorite song in community singing and at camp fires.

Ha-ru-ach no-she-vet k'ri-ra
No-si-fa ki-sam lam-du-ra
V'-chach biz-ro-ot ar-ga-man
Ba-ésh ya-a-le k'-kor-ban
Ha-ésh m'-hav-he-vet shi-ra m'-lav-le-vet
So-vév lo so-vév ha-fin-jan

הָרוּחַ נוֹשֶׁבֶת קְרִירָה
נוֹסִיפָה קִיסָם לַמְּדוּרָה
וְכָךְ בִּזְרוֹעוֹת אַרְגָּמָן
בָּאֵשׁ יַעֲלֶה כְּקָרְבָּן
הָאֵשׁ מְהַבְהֶבֶת שִׁירָה מְלַבְלֶבֶת
סוֹבֵב לוֹ סוֹבֵב הַפִנְגָ'ן

The wind is cool and we feed the fire as it burns, while we sit around it singing, waiting for the coffee in the Finjan to boil. Round and round goes the Finjan.

EREV SHEL SHOSHANIM

Y. Hadar   Lyrics: M. Dor

This is the most widely known song from the pen of Josef Hadar, one of Israel's popular composers. It is so well known that its authorship is often forgotten and is mistakenly thought to be a folk song. *Erev Shel Shoshanim* has become the processional melody for many brides.

© by the authors. All rights reserved

E-rev shel sho-sha-nim né-tsé na el ha-bus-tan
Mor b'sa-mim u-l'vo-na l'-rag-léch mif-tan
Refrain
Lai-la yo-réd l'-at v'-ru-ach sho-shan nosh-va
Ha-va el-chash lach shir ba-lat ze-mer shel a-ha-va

Sha-char ho-ma yo-na ro-shéch ma-lé t'-la-lim
Pich el ha-bo-ker sho-sha-na ek-t'fe-nu li   *Refrain*

עֶרֶב שֶׁל שׁוֹשַׁנִּים נֵצֵא נָא אֶל הַבֻּסְתָּן
מוֹר בְּשָׂמִים וּלְבוֹנָה לְרַגְלֵךְ מִפְתָּן
פזמון
לַיְלָה יוֹרֵד לְאַט וְרוּחַ שׁוֹשָׁן נוֹשְׁבָה
הָבָה אֶלְחַשׁ לָךְ שִׁיר בַּלָּאט זֶמֶר שֶׁל אַהֲבָה

שַׁחַר הוֹמָה יוֹנָה, רֹאשֵׁךְ מָלֵא טְלָלִים
פִּיךְ אֶל הַבֹּקֶר שׁוֹשַׁנָּה אֶקְטְפֶנּוּ לִי פזמון

An evening fragrant with roses. Let us go out to the orchard. Myrrh, spices and frankincense shall be as a threshold for your feet.

T'FILA

Music: A. Bratter   Lyrics: M. Aloni

Hu ha-yo-shév lo é sham bam-ro-mim	הוּא הַיוֹשֵׁב לוֹ אֵי שָׁם בַּמְּרוֹמִים
Hu ha-ro-fe kol cho-lim	הוּא הָרוֹפֵא כָּל חוֹלִים
Hu ha-no-tén rov sim-cha la-y'-la-dim	הוּא הַנּוֹתֵן רֹב שִׂמְחָה לַיְלָדִים
Hu ha-o-se mish-pa-tim	הוּא הָעוֹשֶׂה מִשְׁפָּטִים
Hu ba-sha-ma-yim v'-hu ha-ya-chid	הוּא בַּשָּׁמַיִם וְהוּא הַיָּחִיד
Hu ha-ga-dol ha-no-ra	הוּא הַגָּדוֹל הַנּוֹרָא
Hu ha-sho-mér a-lé-nu mi-tsa-ra	הוּא הַשּׁוֹמֵר עָלֵינוּ מִצָּרָה
E-lo-ha	אֱלוֹהַּ
Sh'-mor na a-lé-nu k'-mo y'-la-dim	שְׁמוֹר נָא עָלֵינוּ כְּמוֹ יְלָדִים
Sh'-mor na v'-al ta-a-zov	שְׁמוֹר נָא וְאַל תַּעֲזֹב
Tén la-nu or v'-sim-chat n'-u-rim	תֵּן לָנוּ אוֹר וְשִׂמְחַת נְעוּרִים
Tén la-nu ko-ach od va-od	תֵּן לָנוּ כֹּחַ עוֹד וָעוֹד
Tén la-nu gam le-e-hov	תֵּן לָנוּ גַּם לֶאֱהוֹב

He who sits in the heavens heals the sick, gives joy to children and is our protector from pain—God. Watch over us as children and don't leave us. Give us light and the joy of youth. Give us strength and the ability to love.

ZEMER ATIK

Music: A. Neeman   Lyrics M. Kashtan

©Edition Negen, ACUM Israel

Od na-shu-va el ni-gun a-tik	עוֹד נָשׁוּבָה אֶל נִגּוּן עַתִּיק
V'-ha-ze-mer yif v'-ye-e-rav	וְהַזֶּמֶר יִיף וְיֶעֱרַב
Od ga-vi-a m'-shu-mar na-shik	עוֹד גָּבִיעַ מְשֻׁמָּר נָשִׁיק
A-li-zé é-na-yim v'-lé-vav	עַלִּיזֵי עֵינַיִם וְלֵבָב
To-vu o-ha-lé-nu	טוֹבוּ, טוֹבוּ אֹהָלֵינוּ
Ki ma-chol hif-tsi-a	כִּי מָחוֹל הִפְצִיעַ
To-vu o-ha-lé-nu	טוֹבוּ, טוֹבוּ אֹהָלֵינוּ
Od na-shu-va el ni-gun a-tik	עוֹד נָשׁוּבָה אֶל נִגּוּן עַתִּיק

We shall yet return to the old sweet tune and break forth in dance.

TSENA

I. Miron & J. Grossman
Lyrics: Y. Hagiz

The original melody was written by Issachar Miron while the third part of the round was added by Julius Grossman. In this combination the song became a runaway international hit when recorded by the Weavers in the early 1950's. Millions of copies of this recording (flip side -- Irene Good Night) were sold and the tune became a household item among non-Jews as well as Jews.

© by the authors. All rights reserved

Tse-na ha-ba-not ur'-e-na
Cha-ya-lim ba-mo-sha-va
Al na tit-cha-be-na
Mi-ben cha-yil ish tsa-va

צְאֶנָה הַבָּנוֹת וּרְאֶינָה
חַיָלִים בַּמוֹשָׁבָה
אַל נָא תִּתְחַבֵּנָה
מִבֶּן חַיִל אִישׁ צָבָא

Come out, you fair girls, and greet the soldiers. Do not fear the heroic warriors.

RAD HALAILA

Hassidic   Lyrics: Y. Orland

Like many Israeli songs of the early 20th century, **Rad Halaila**, is an old Hassidic melody. It was given renewed life with the addition of the Hebrew lyrics by Yaakov Orland and has become one of the most popular Hora melodies.

©Tarbut Vechinuch Ed., ACUM Israel

42

Rad ha-lai-la rav shi-ré-nu
Ha-bo-ké-a la-sha-ma-yim
Shu-vi ho-ra-té-nu
M'-chu-de-shet shiv-a-ta-yim
Shu-vi v'-na-sov
Ki dar-ké-nu én la sof
Ki od nim-she-chet ha-shal-she-let
Ki li-bé-nu lév e-chad
Mé-o-lam v'-a-dé ad
Ki od nim-she-chet ha-shal-she-let

רַד הַלַּיְלָה רַב שִׁירֵנוּ
הַבּוֹקֵעַ לַשָּׁמַיִם
שׁוּבִי הוֹרָתֵנוּ
מְחֻדֶּשֶׁת שִׁבְעָתַיִם
שׁוּבִי וְנָסֹב
כִּי דַרְכֵּנוּ אֵין לָה סוֹף
כִּי עוֹד נִמְשֶׁכֶת הַשַּׁלְשֶׁלֶת
כִּי לִבֵּנוּ לֵב אֶחָד
מֵעוֹלָם וְעֲדֵי עַד
כִּי עוֹד נִמְשֶׁכֶת הַשַּׁלְשֶׁלֶת

The night descends and our songs pierce the skies. Hora, return to us sevenfold. Our heart was always one heart and the chain will ever continue—never to be broken.

HAKOTEL

Music: D. Seltzer Lyrics: J. Gamzu

When the Western Wall, sacred to Judaism since ancient times, was recaptured and placed once again in Jewish hands, Dov Seltzer's moving song was heard throughout the land and abroad.

© by the authors. All rights reserved

Am-da na-a-ra mul ha-ko-tel	עָמְדָה נַעֲרָה מוּל הַכֹּתֶל
S'-fa-ta-yim kér-va v'-san-tér	שְׂפָתַיִם קְרֵבָה וְסַנְטֵר
Am-ra li t'-ki-ot ha-sho-far cha-za-kot hén	אָמְרָה לִי תְּקִיעוֹת הַשּׁוֹפָר חֲזָקוֹת הֵן
A-val ha-sh'ti-ka od yo-tér	אֲבָל הַשְּׁתִיקָה עוֹד יוֹתֵר
Am-ra li Tsi-yon har ha-ba-yit	אָמְרָה לִי צִיּוֹן הַר הַבַּיִת
Shat-ka li ha-g'mul v'-ha-z'chut	שָׁתְקָה לִי הַגְּמוּל וְהַזְּכוּת
U-ma she-za-har al mits-cha bén ar-ba-yim	וּמַה שֶּׁזָּהַר עַל מִצְחָהּ בֵּין עַרְבַּיִם
Ha-ya ar-ga-man shel mal-chut	הָיָה אַרְגָּמָן שֶׁל מַלְכוּת
Refrain	פזמון
Ha-ko-tel é-zov v'-a-tse-vet	הַכֹּתֶל אֵזוֹב וְעַצֶּבֶת
Ha-ko-tel o-fe-ret va-dam	הַכֹּתֶל עוֹפֶרֶת וָדָם
Yésh a-na-shim im lév shel e-ven	יֵשׁ אֲנָשִׁים עִם לֵב שֶׁל אֶבֶן
Yésh a-na-shim im lé a-dam	יֵשׁ אֲבָנִים עִם לֵב אָדָם
A-mad ha-tsan-chan mul ha-ko-tel	עָמַד הַצַּנְחָן מוּל הַכֹּתֶל
Mi-kol mach-lak-to rak e-chad	מִכָּל מַחְלַקְתּוֹ רַק אֶחָד
A-mar li "la-ma-vet én d'-mut ach yésh ko-ter—	אָמַר לִי לַמָּוֶת אֵין דְּמוּת אַךְ יֵשׁ קֹטֶר
Tish-a mi-li-me-ter bil-vad"	תִּשְׁעָה מִילִימֶטֶר בִּלְבַד
A-mar li "é-ne-ni do-mé-a"	אָמַר לִי אֵינֶנִּי דּוֹמֵעַ
(V'shav l'-hash-pil ma-ba-tim)	(וְשָׁב לְהַשְׁפִּיל מַבָּטִים)
"Ach sa-ba she-li E-lo-him ha-yo-dé-a	אַךְ סַבָּא שֶׁלִּי אֱלֹהִים הַיּוֹדֵעַ
Ka-vur kan b'-har ha-zé-tim"	קָבוּר כָּאן בְּהַר הַזֵּיתִים
Refrain	פזמון
Am-da bish-cho-rim mul ha-ko-tel	עָמְדָה בִּשְׁחוֹרִים מוּל הַכֹּתֶל
I-mo shel e-chad min ha-chir	אִמּוֹ שֶׁל אֶחָד מִן הַחַיִ״ר
Am-ra li "é-né na-a-ri ha-dol-kot hén	אָמְרָה לִי עֵינֵי נַעֲרִי הַדּוֹלְקוֹת הֵן
V'-lo ha-né-rot she-ba-kir"	וְלֹא הַנֵּרוֹת שֶׁבַּקִּיר
Am-ra li "é-ne-ni ro-she-met	אָמְרָה לִי אֵינֶנִּי רוֹשֶׁמֶת
Shum pe-tek lit-mon bén s'-da-kav	שׁוּם פֶּתֶק לִטְמוֹן בֵּין סְדָקָיו
Ki ma she-na-ta-ti la-ko-tel rak e-mesh	כִּי מַה שֶּׁנָּתַתִּי לַכֹּתֶל רַק אֶמֶשׁ
Ga-dol mi-mi-lim u-mich-tav"	גָּדוֹל מִמִּלִּים וּמִכְתָּב
Refrain	פזמון

A young girl, a paratrooper and a mother stand leaning against the Western Wall each deep in thought. There are people with hearts of stone; there are stones with human hearts.

EL GINAT EGOZ

Music: S. Levi-Tanai
Lyrics: Song of Songs 6:11, 8:12

©by the Author. All rights reserved

El gi-nat e-goz ya-ra-d'-ti
Li-r'-ot b'-i-bé ha-na-chal
Li-r'-ot ha-fa-r'-cha ha-ge-fen
Hé-né-tsu ha-ri-mo-nim

אֶל גִּנַּת אֱגוֹז יָרַדְתִּי
לִרְאוֹת בְּאִבֵּי הַנָּחַל
לִרְאוֹת הֲפָרְחָה הַגֶּפֶן
הֵנֵצוּ הָרִמּוֹנִים

I went down to the garden of nuts to look at the green plants, of the valley to see whether the vine budded and the pomegranates were in flower.

MA AVARECH

Music: Y. Rosenblum Lyrics: R. Shapira

© by the authors. All rights reserved

Refrain
Ma a-va-réch lo ba-me y'-vo-rach
Ze ha-ye-led sha-al ha-mal-ach

U-vé-rach lo chi-yuch she-ka-mo-hu ka-or
U-vé-rach lo é-na-yim g'-do-lot v'-ro-ot
Lit-pos ban kol pe-rach v'-chai v'-tsi-por
V'-lév l'-har-gish bo et kol ha-mar-ot *Refrain*

U-vé-rach lo rag-la-yim lir-kod ad én sof
V'-ne-fesh liz-kor ba et kol hal-cha-nim
V'-yad ha-o-se-fet ts'-da-fim a-lé chof
V'-o-zen k'-shu-va lig-do-lim uk'-ta-nim *Refrain*

U-vé-rach ki ya-dav ha-l'-mu-dot bif-ra-chim
Yits-l'-chu gam lil-mod et ots-mat hap-la-da
V'-rag-lav ha-rok-dot et ma-sa had-ra-chim
Us-fa-tav ha-sha-rot et mik-tsav hap-ku-da

פזמון
מַה אֲבָרֵךְ לוֹ בַּמֶּה יְבֹרַךְ
זֶה הַיֶּלֶד שָׁאַל הַמַּלְאָךְ

וּבֵרַךְ לוֹ חִיּוּךְ שֶׁכָּמוֹהוּ כָּאוֹר
וּבֵרַךְ לוֹ עֵינַיִם גְּדוֹלוֹת וְרוֹאוֹת
לִתְפֹּס בָּן כָּל פֶּרַח וְחַי וְצִפּוֹר
וְלֵב לְהַרְגִּישׁ בּוֹ אֶת כָּל הַמַּרְאוֹת פזמון

וּבֵרַךְ לוֹ רַגְלַיִם לִרְקוֹד עַד אֵין סוֹף
וְנֶפֶשׁ לִזְכֹּר בָּהּ אֶת כָּל הַלְּחָנִים
וְיַד הָאוֹסֶפֶת צְדָפִים עֲלֵי חוֹף
וְאֹזֶן קְשׁוּבָה לִגְדוֹלִים וּקְטַנִּים פזמון

וּבֵרַךְ כִּי יָדָיו הַלִּמּוּדוֹת בִּפְרָחִים
יִצְלְחוּ גַּם לִלְמֹד אֶת עָצְמַת הַפְּלָדָה
וְרַגְלָיו הָרוֹקְדוֹת אֶת מַסַּע הַדְּרָכִים
וּשְׂפָתָיו הַשָּׁרוֹת אֶת מִקְצַב הַפְּקֻדָּה

"How shall this child be blessed?" the angel asked. And he blessed him
with a smile and with eyes that could see all living things; and with a
heart that could feel all that is seen.

AL KOL ÉLE

N. Shemer

Just as "Jerusalem of Gold" became synonymous with the War of 1967, **Al Kol Ele** was associated with the 1982 war in Lebanon. It has since become one of Naomi Shemer's most beloved songs and it's theme of hope and faith is as meaningful today as it was when first composed.

Al ha-dvash v'-al ha-o-kets	עַל הַדְּבַשׁ וְעַל הָעוֹקֶץ
Al ha-mar v'-ha-ma-tok	עַל הַמַּר וְהַמָּתוֹק
Al bi-té-nu ha-ti-no-ket	עַל בִּתֵּנוּ הַתִּינוֹקֶת
Sh'-mor É-li ha-tov	שְׁמוֹר אֵלִי הַטּוֹב
Al ha-ésh ha-m'-vo-e-ret	עַל הָאֵשׁ הַמְבוֹעֶרֶת
Al ha-ma-yim ha-za-kim	עַל הַמַּיִם הַזַּכִּים
Al ha-ish ha-shav ha-baita	עַל הָאִישׁ הַשָּׁב הַבַּיְתָה
Min ha-mer-cha-kim	מִן הַמֶּרְחַקִּים
Al kol é-le, al kol é-le	עַל כָּל אֵלֶּה עַל כָּל אֵלֶּה
Sh'-mor na li É-li ha-tov	שְׁמוֹר נָא לִי אֵלִי הַטּוֹב
Al ha-dvash v'-al ha-o-kets	עַל הַדְּבַשׁ וְעַל הָעוֹקֶץ
Al ha-mar v'-ha-ma-tok	עַל הַמַּר וְהַמָּתוֹק
Al na ta-a-kor na-tu-a	אַל נָא תַעֲקוֹר נָטוּעַ
Al tish-kach et ha-tik-va	אַל תִּשְׁכַּח אֶת הַתִּקְוָה
Ha-shi-vé-ni v'-a-shu-va	הֲשִׁיבֵנִי וְאָשׁוּבָה
El ha-a-rets ha-to-va	אֶל הָאָרֶץ הַטּוֹבָה

Through the sting and through the honey through the bitter and the sweet do not destroy my hope, my yearning. Bring me back and I will return to the good land.

MACHAR

N. Shemer

Ma-char u-lai naf-li-ga ba-sfi-not	מָחָר אוּלַי נַפְלִיגָה בַּסְפִינוֹת
Mé-chof E-lat ad chof shen-hav	מֵחוֹף אֵילַת עַד חוֹף שֶׁנְהָב
V'-al ha-mash-cha-tot ha-y'-sha-not	וְעַל הַמַּשְׁחָתוֹת הַיְשָׁנוֹת
Yat-i-nu ta-pu-ché za-hav	יַטְעִינוּ טַפּוּחֵי זָהָב
Refrain	פזמון
Kol ze é-no ma-shal v'-lo cha-lom	כָּל זֶה אֵינוֹ מָשָׁל וְלֹא חֲלוֹם
Ze na-chon ka-or ba-tso-ho-ra-yim	זֶה נָכוֹן כָּאוֹר בַּצָּהֳרַיִם
Kol ze ya-vo ma-char im lo ha-yom	כָּל זֶה יָבוֹא מָחָר אִם לֹא הַיּוֹם
V'-im lo ma-char az moch-ro-ta-yim	וְאִם לֹא מָחָר אָז מָחֳרָתַיִם
Ma-char u-lai b'-chol ha-mish-o-lim	מָחָר אוּלַי בְּכָל הַמִּשְׁעוֹלִים
A-ri b'-é-der tson yin-hag	אֲרִי בְּעֵדֶר צֹאן יִנְהַג
Ma-char ya-ku b'-e-lef in-ba-lim	מָחָר יַכּוּ בְּאֶלֶף עִנְבָּלִים
Ha-mon pa-a-mo-nim shel chag *Refrain*	הֲמוֹן פַּעֲמוֹנִים שֶׁל חַג פזמון
Machar ya-ku-mu e-lef shi-ku-nim	מָחָר יָקוּמוּ אֶלֶף שִׁכּוּנִים
V'-shir ya-uf ba-mir-pa-sot	וְשִׁיר יָעוּף בַּמִּרְפָּסוֹת
U-shlal ka-la-ni-yot v'-tsiv-o-nim	וּשְׁלַל כַּלָּנִיּוֹת וְצִבְעוֹנִים
Ya-a-lu mi-toch ha-ha-ri-sot *Refrain*	יַעֲלוּ מִתּוֹךְ הַהֲרִיסוֹת פזמון
Ma-char k'-she-ha-tsa-va yif-shot ma-dav	מָחָר כְּשֶׁהַצָּבָא יִפְשֹׁט מַדָּיו
Li-bé-nu ya-a-vor l'-dom	לִבֵּנוּ יַעֲבֹר לְדֹם
A-char kol ish yiv-ne bish-té ya-dav	אַחַר כָּל אִישׁ יִבְנֶה בִּשְׁתֵּי יָדָיו
Et ma she-hu cha-lam ha-yom *Refrain*	אֶת מַה שֶׁהוּא חָלַם הַיּוֹם פזמון
V'-im od lo machar (3) az moch-ro-ta-yim	וְאִם עוֹד לֹא מָחָר(3) אָז מָחֳרָתַיִם

Tomorrow will bring a new dawn of peace. And if not tomorrow then surely the following day.

HAMILCHAMA HA'ACHRONA

Music: D. Seltzer   Lyrics: H. Hefer

Composed during the Yom Kippur War period in 1973, this song was widely sung in Israel and in many Jewish communities throughout the world. Its plaintive mood, unlike the ebullience of the songs resulting from the 1967 Six Day War, expresses the determination that this, the Yom Kippur War, shall be the last of all the conflicts.

zo ti-h'-ye ha-mil-cha-ma ha-ach-ro-na

© by the authors. All rights reserved

B'-shém kol ha-tank-is-tim
Uf-né-hem ha-m'-u-va-kot
A-sher av-ru et kol
Ha-ésh v'-hash-chi-kot
B'-shém ha-ya-ma-im
A-sher pash-tu al ha-n'-ma-lim
V'-é-né-hem k'-vé-dot
Mi-me-lach v'-ga-lim

Refrain
A-ni mav-ti-ach lach
Yal-da she-li k'-ta-na
She-zo ti-ye
Ha-mil-cha-ma ha-ach-ro-na

B'-shém ha-ta-ya-sim
A-sher par-tsu el k'-rav zo-ém
V'-nits-r'-vu ba-ésh ti-lim v'-ésh nun mem
B'-shém ha-tsan-cha-nim she-bén o-fe-ret v'-a-shan
R'-u o-tach k'-mo mal-ach mé-al ro-sham *Refrain*

B'-shém ha-tot-cha-nim
A-sher b'-re-sek hap-ga-zim
Ha-yu a-mud ha-ésh l'-o-rech ha-cha-zit
B'-shém chov-shim rof'-im
She-b'-naf-sham u-m'-o-dam
Hech-zi-ru ru-ach v'-cha-yim hé-shi-vu-dam *Refrain*

B'-shém ha-ka-sha-rim a-sher ko-lam ka-ra lé-lot
B'-shém kol ha-ga-ya-sot v'-ha-cha-ya-lot
B'-shém kol ha-a-vot a-sher hal-chu lak-rav no-ra
V'-she-ro-tsim la-shuv é-la-yich cha-za-ra *Refrain*

בְּשֵׁם כָּל הַתַּנְקִסְתִּים
וּפְנֵיהֶם הַמְאוּבָּקוֹת
אֲשֶׁר עָבְרוּ אֶת כָּל
הָאֵשׁ וְהַשְּׁחִיקוֹת
בְּשֵׁם הַיַּמָּאִים
אֲשֶׁר פָּשְׁטוּ עַל הַנְּמָלִים
וְעֵינֵיהֶם כְּבֵדוֹת
מִמֶּלַח וְגַלִּים

פזמון
אֲנִי מַבְטִיחַ לָךְ
יַלְדָּה שֶׁלִּי קְטַנָּה
שֶׁזּוּ תִּהְיֶה
הַמִּלְחָמָה הָאַחֲרוֹנָה

בְּשֵׁם הַטַּיָּסִים
אֲשֶׁר פָּרְצוּ אֶל קְרָב זוֹעֵם
וְנִצְרְבוּ בָּאֵשׁ טִילִים וְאֵשׁ נוּן-מֶם
בְּשֵׁם הַצַּנְחָנִים שֶׁבֵּין עוֹפֶרֶת וְעָשָׁן
רָאוּ אוֹתָךְ כְּמוֹ מַלְאָךְ מֵעַל רֹאשָׁם פזמון

בְּשֵׁם הַתּוֹתְחָנִים
אֲשֶׁר בְּרֶסֶק הַפְּגָזִים
הָיוּ עַמּוּד הָאֵשׁ לְאֹרֶךְ הַחֲזִית
בְּשֵׁם חוֹבְשִׁים רוֹפְאִים
שֶׁבְּנַפְשָׁם וּמְאוֹדָם
הֶחֱזִירוּ רוּחַ וְחַיִּים הֵשִׁיבוּ דָּם (פזמון)

בְּשֵׁם הַקַּשָּׁרִים אֲשֶׁר קוֹלָם קָרָא לֵילוֹת
בְּשֵׁם כָּל הַגַּיָּסוֹת וְהַחַיָּילוֹת
בְּשֵׁם כָּל הָאָבוֹת אֲשֶׁר הָלְכוּ לַקְרָב נוֹרָא
וְשֶׁרוֹצִים לָשׁוּב אֵלַיִךְ חֲזָרָה פזמון

In the name of the entire armed forces who have been through the raging battle, I promise you, my little girl, that this shall be the last war.

LACH Y'RUSHALAYIM

Music: E. Rubinstein   Lyrics: A. Etinger

The repertoire of Israeli songs is replete with melodies dedicated to the city of Jerusalem. This city has been the focal point of all prayers for 2000 years of the Jewish diaspora. This version appeared after the Six Day War and its spirited lilt shows the new and proud feeling with regard to a returned Jerusalem.

© Edition Paamonim

Lach Y'-ru-sha-la-yim bén cho-mot ha-ir
Lach Y'-ru-sha-la-yim or cha-dash ya-ir
Refrain
B'-li-bé-nu rak shir e-chad ka-yam
Lach Y'-ru-sha-la-yim bén Yar-dén va-yam

Lach Y'-ru-sha-la-yim lach k'-du-mim va-hod
Lach y'-ru-sha-la-yim lach ra-zim va-sod *Refrain*

Lach Y'-ru-sha-la-yim shir ni-sa ta-mid
Lach Y'-ru-sha-la-yim ir mig-dal Da-vid *Refrain*

לָךְ יְרוּשָׁלַיִם בֵּין חוֹמוֹת הָעִיר
לָךְ יְרוּשָׁלַיִם אוֹר חָדָשׁ יָאִיר
פזמון
בְּלִבֵּנוּ רַק שִׁיר אֶחָד קַיָּם
לָךְ יְרוּשָׁלַיִם בֵּין יַרְדֵּן וָיָם

לָךְ יְרוּשָׁלַיִם לָךְ קְדוּמִים וָהוֹד
לָךְ יְרוּשָׁלַיִם לָךְ רָזִים וָסוֹד פזמון

לָךְ יְרוּשָׁלַיִם שִׁיר נִישָׂא תָּמִיד
לָךְ יְרוּשָׁלַיִם עִיר מִגְדַּל דָּוִד פזמון

For you, O Jerusalem, fortress of David, let a new light shine. In our hearts there exists but one song, a song dedicated to you.

JERUSALEM OF GOLD

Y'RUSHALAYIM SHEL ZAHAV

N. Shemer

Without doubt this was the most important and widely heard song in the immediate aftermath of the Six Day War. It was introduced at the yearly Song Festival presented as the climax to Israel Independence Day and was sung by Shuli Natan. With the retaking of the old city of Jerusalem and the return of the sacred Western Wall, the song assumed additional emotional appeal. Within a period of days following the Six Day War the song was recorded by a number of artists both in Israel and in the United States. The song became known throughout the world wherever Jews reside.

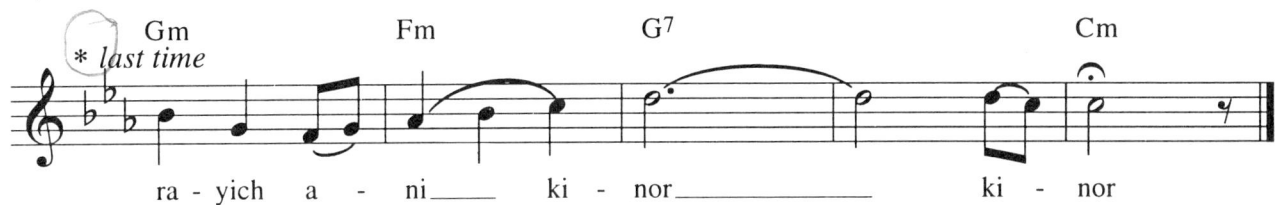

A-vir ha-rim tsa-lul ka-ya-yin v'-ré-ach o-ra-nim	אֲוִיר הָרִים צָלוּל כַּיַּיִן וְרֵיחַ אוֹרָנִים
Ni-sa b'-ru-ach ha-ar-ba-yim im kol pa-a-mo-nim	נִשָּׂא בְּרוּחַ הָעַרְבַּיִם עִם קוֹל פַּעֲמוֹנִים
Uv-tar-dé-mat i-lan va-e-ven sh'-vu-ya ba-cha-lo-ma	וּבְתַרְדֵּמַת אִילָן וָאֶבֶן שְׁבוּיָה בַּחֲלוֹמָה
Ha-ir a-sher ba-dad yo-she-vet u-v'-li-ba cho-ma	הָעִיר אֲשֶׁר בָּדָד יוֹשֶׁבֶת וּבְלִבָּהּ חוֹמָה
Refrain	פזמון
Y'-ru-sha-la-yim shel za-hav v'shel n'cho-shet v'shel or	יְרוּשָׁלַיִם שֶׁל זָהָב וְשֶׁל נְחֹשֶׁת וְשֶׁל אוֹר
Ha-lo l'chol shi-ra-yich a-ni ki-nor	הֲלֹא לְכָל שִׁירַיִךְ אֲנִי כִּנּוֹר

Cha-zar-nu el bo-rot ha-ma-yim la-shuk v'-la-ki-kar	חָזַרְנוּ אֶל בּוֹרוֹת הַמַּיִם לַשּׁוּק וְלַכִּכָּר
Sho-far ko-ré b'-har ha-ba-yit ba-ir ha-a-ti-ka	שׁוֹפָר קוֹרֵא בְּהַר הַבַּיִת בָּעִיר הָעַתִּיקָה
U-vam-a-rot a-sher ba-se-la al-fé shma-shot zor-chot	וּבַמְּעָרוֹת אֲשֶׁר בַּסֶּלַע אַלְפֵי שְׁמָשׁוֹת זוֹרְחוֹת
V'shuv né-réd el yam ha-me-lach b'-de-rech Y'-ri-cho	וְשׁוּב נֵרֵד אֶל יָם הַמֶּלַח בְּדֶרֶךְ יְרִיחוֹ פזמון
Refrain	

Ach b'-vo-i ha-yom la-shir lach	אַךְ בְּבוֹאִי הַיּוֹם לָשִׁיר לָךְ
V'-lach lik-shor k'ta-rim	וְלָךְ לִקְשׁוֹר כְּתָרִים
Ka-ton-ti mi-ts'-ir ba-na-yich	קָטֹנְתִּי מִצְּעִיר בָּנַיִךְ
U-mé-a-cha-ron ham-sho-r'-rim	וּמֵאַחֲרוֹן הַמְשׁוֹרְרִים
Ki shméch tso-rév et has-fa-ta-yim	כִּי שְׁמֵךְ צוֹרֵב אֶת הַשְּׂפָתַיִם
K'-n'-shi-kat sa-raf	כִּנְשִׁיקַת שָׂרָף
Im esh-ka-chéch Y'-ru-sha-la-yim	אִם אֶשְׁכָּחֵךְ יְרוּשָׁלַיִם
A-sher ku-la za-hav	אֲשֶׁר כֻּלָּהּ זָהָב
Refrain	פזמון

Jerusalem of gold, of copper and of light, I shall accompany all the songs dedicated to you.

HAL'LUYA

S. Or & K. Oshrat

This was the winning song in the 1979 Eurovision Song Festival. It was recorded in an English version by Steve Lawrence and Eydie Gorme under the name of "Parker and Penny."

Moderately

Ha-l'-lu-ya la-o-lam ha-l'-lu-ya ya-shi-ru ku-lam b'-mi-la a-chat bo-dé-da ha-lév ma-lë ba-ha-mon to-da v'-ho-lém gam hu é-ze o-lam nif-la ha-l'-lu-ya im ha-shir ha-l'-lu-ya al yom she-mé-ir ha-l'-lu-ya al ma she-ha-ya ya u-ma she-od lo ha-ya ha-l'-lu-ya

© by the authors. All rights reserved.

Ha-l'-lu-ya la-o-lam	הַלְלוּיָה לָעוֹלָם
Ha-l'-lu-ya ya-shi-ru ku-lam	הַלְלוּיָה יָשִׁירוּ כֻּלָם
B'-mi-la a-chat bo-dé-da	בְּמִלָה אַחַת בּוֹדְדָה
Ha-lév ma-lé b'-ha-mon to-da	הַלֵב מָלֵא בַּהֲמוֹן תוֹדָה
V'-ho-lém gam hu é-ze o-lam nif-la	וְהוֹלֵם גַם הוּא אֵיזֶה עוֹלָם נִפְלָא
Ha-l'-lu-ya im ha-shir	הַלְלוּיָה עִם הַשִׁיר
Ha-l'-lu-ya al yom she-mé-ir	הַלְלוּיָה עַל יוֹם שֶׁמֵאִיר
Ha-l'-lu-ya al ma she-ha-ya	הַלְלוּיָה עַל מַה שֶׁהָיָה
U-ma she-od lo ha-ya	וּמַה שֶׁעוֹד לֹא הָיָה
Ha-l'-lu-ya	הַלְלוּיָה

Sing Haleluya to the world. Sing Haleluya to a bright new day. Haleluya for that which was–and for all that will be. Haleluya!

CHAI

Music: A. Toledano Lyrics: E. Manor

This song launched the international career of Ofra Haza when she sang it in the Eurovision competition. The phrase *am Yisrael chai* is sometimes substituted in the refrain.

© by the authors. All rights reserved

Shim-u a-chai a-ni od chai	שִׁמְעוּ אַחַי אֲנִי עוֹד חַי
Ush'-té é-nai od ni-sa-ot la-or	וּשְׁתֵּי עֵינַי עוֹד נְשׂוּאוֹת לָאוֹר
Ra-bim cho-chai ach gam pra-chai	רַבִּים חוֹכַי אַךְ גַּם פְּרָחַי
U-l'-fa-nai sha-nim ra-bot mis-for	וּלְפָנַי שָׁנִים רַבּוֹת מִסְפּוֹר
A-ni sho-él u-mit-pa-lél	אֲנִי שׁוֹאֵל וּמִתְפַּלֵּל
Tov she-lo av-da od ha-tik-va	טוֹב שֶׁלֹּא אָבְדָה עוֹד הַתִּקְוָה
O-vér miz-mor mi-dor l'-dor	עוֹבֵר מִזְמוֹר מִדּוֹר לְדוֹר
K'-ma'-yan mé-az v'-ad o-lam	כְּמַעְיָן מֵאָז וְעַד עוֹלָם
A-ni sho-él u-mit-pa-lél	אֲנִי שׁוֹאֵל וּמִתְפַּלֵּל
Tov she-lo av-da od ha-tik-va	טוֹב שֶׁלֹּא אָבְדָה עוֹד הַתִּקְוָה
Refrain	פזמון
Chai, chai, chai	חַי חַי חַי
Kén a-ni od chai	כֵּן אֲנִי עוֹד חַי
Ze ha-shir she-sa-ba	זֶה הַשִּׁיר שֶׁסַּבָּא
Shar et-mol l'-a-ba	שָׁר אֶתְמוֹל לְאַבָּא
V'-ha-yom a-ni	וְהַיּוֹם אֲנִי
Ani od	אֲנִי עוֹד
Refrain	פזמון

Listen brothers! I'm still alive! Alive, alive, indeed I am alive! The people of Israel are alive. How wonderful that hope is never lost.

NOLAD'TI L'SHALOM

U. Hitman

A-ni no-la-d'-ti	אֲנִי נוֹלַדְתִּי
El ha-man-gi-not	אֶל הַמַּנְגִּינוֹת
V'-el ha-shi-rim	וְאֶל הַשִּׁירִים
Shel kol ha-m'-di-not	שֶׁל כָּל הַמְּדִינוֹת
No-la-d'-ti la-la-shon	נוֹלַדְתִּי לַלָּשׁוֹן
V'-gam la-ma-kom	וְגַם לַמָּקוֹם
La-m'-at l'-ha-mon	לַמְעַט לֶהָמוֹן
She-yo-sheet yad la-sha-lom	שֶׁיּוֹשִׁיט יָד לַשָּׁלוֹם
Ah....................	אה....................
A-ni no-la-d'-ti la-sha-lom	אֲנִי נוֹלַדְתִּי לַשָּׁלוֹם
She-rak ya-gi-a	שֶׁרַק יַגִּיעַ
A-ni no-la-d'-ti la-sha-lom	אֲנִי נוֹלַדְתִּי לַשָּׁלוֹם
She- rak ya-vo	שֶׁרַק יָבוֹא
A-ni no-la-d'-ti la-sha-lom	אֲנִי נוֹלַדְתִּי לַשָּׁלוֹם
She-rak yo-fi-a	שֶׁרַק יוֹפִיעַ
A-ni ro-tse ani ro-tse	אֲנִי רוֹצָה אֲנִי רוֹצָה
Li-yot k'-var bo	לִהְיוֹת כְּבָר בּוֹ

I was born to the themes and the songs of all countries. I was born to the language and also to the place, to the few and to the many and will stretch out a hand to peace.

Y'RUSHALAYIM

Folktune   Lyrics: A. Hameiri

This well known song has a permanent place in the repertoire of Israeli song. Although the authorship of the melody is not known, Avigdor Hameiri's words directed to the city of Jerusalem have made it a long standing favorite.

Mé-al pis-gat har ha-tso-fim	מֵעַל פִּסְגַּת הַר הַצּוֹפִים
Esh-ta-cha-ve lach a-pa-yim	אֶשְׁתַּחֲוֶה לָךְ אַפַּיִם
Mé-al pis-gat har ha-tso-fim	מֵעַל פִּסְגַּת הַר הַצּוֹפִים
Sha-lom lach Y'ru-sha-la-yim	שָׁלוֹם לָךְ יְרוּשָׁלַיִם
Mé-a do-rot cha-lam-ti a-la-yich	מֵאָה דוֹרוֹת חָלַמְתִּי עָלַיִךְ
Liz-kot lir-ot b'or pa-na-yich	לִזְכּוֹת לִרְאוֹת בְּאוֹר פָּנַיִךְ
Y'-ru-sha-la-yim, Y'-ru-sha-la-yim	יְרוּשָׁלַיִם יְרוּשָׁלַיִם
Ha-i-ri pa-na-yich liv-néch	הָאִירִי פָּנַיִךְ לִבְנֵךְ
Y'-ru-sha-la-yim, Y'-rusha-la-yim	יְרוּשָׁלַיִם יְרוּשָׁלַיִם
Mé-chor-vo-ta-yich ev-néch	מֵחָרְבוֹתַיִךְ אֶבְנֵךְ

From atop Mount Scopus we greet you, O Jerusalem. For a hundred generations we dreamed of your beauty. Jerusalem, we shall once again rebuild you.

SISU ET Y'RUSHALAYIM

Music: A. Nof   Lyrics: Isaiah

Sisu Et Y'rushalayim entered the Israeli musical scene via a Hassidic Song Festival. With text based on a number of far flung verses in Isaiah, Akiva Nof has fashioned a song which has proved durable. It is popular in many areas where Jews reside.

©by the Author. All rights reserved

Refrain
Si-su et Y'ru-sha-la-yim gi-lu va
Gi-lu va kol o-ha-ve-ha

Al cho-mo-ta-yich ir Da-vid hif-ka-d'-ti shom-rim
Kol ha-yom v'-chol ha-lai-la *Refrain*

Al ti-ra v'al té-chat av-di Ya-a-kov
Ki ya-fu-tsu m'-san-e-cha mi-pa-ne-cha *Refrain*

S'-i sa-viv é-na-yich u-r'-i ku-lam
Nik'-b'-tsu u-va-u lach *Refrain*

V'-a-méch ku-lam tsa-di-kim
L'-o-lam yir-shu a-rets *Refrain*

פזמון
שִׂישׂוּ אֶת יְרוּשָׁלַיִם גִּילוּ בָה
גִּילוּ בָה כָּל אוֹהֲבֶיהָ

עַל חוֹמוֹתַיִךְ עִיר דָּוִד הִפְקַדְתִּי שׁוֹמְרִים
כָּל הַיּוֹם וְכָל הַלַּיְלָה פזמון

אַל תִּירָא וְאַל תֵּחַת עַבְדִּי יַעֲקֹב
כִּי יָפוּצוּ מְשַׂנְאֶיךָ מִפָּנֶיךָ פזמון

שְׂאִי סָבִיב עֵינַיִךְ וּרְאִי כֻלָּם
נִקְבְּצוּ וּבָאוּ לָךְ פזמון

וְעַמֵּךְ כֻּלָּם צַדִּיקִים
לְעוֹלָם יִירְשׁוּ אָרֶץ פזמון

Rejoice with Jerusalem all you who love her. I have set watchmen upon the walls O, Jerusalem.

HATIKVAH

Music: Folk   Lyrics: N. H. Imber

Hatikvah was formally declared the Zionist anthem during the 18th Zionist Congress in Prague, 1933. At the Declaration of the State on May 14, 1948, it was sung by the assembly during the opening ceremony and played by members of the Palestine Symphony Orchestra at its conclusion. Both the melody and words have been slightly altered since the establishment of the State of Israel. The version presented here is the official version.

Kol od ba-lé-vav p'-ni-ma	כָּל עוֹד בַּלֵּבָב פְּנִימָה
Nefesh y'-hu-di ho-mi-ya	נֶפֶשׁ יְהוּדִי הוֹמִיָּה
Ul'-fa-té miz-rach ka-di-ma	וּלְפַאֲתֵי מִזְרָח קָדִימָה
A-yin l'-tsi-yon tso-fi-ya	עַיִן לְצִיּוֹן צוֹפִיָּה
Od lo av-da tik-va-té-nu	עוֹד לֹא אָבְדָה תִּקְוָתֵנוּ
Hatikva bat sh'-not al-pa-yim	הַתִּקְוָה בַּת שְׁנוֹת אַלְפַּיִם
Li-yot am chof-shi b'-ar-tsé-nu	לִהְיוֹת עַם חָפְשִׁי בְּאַרְצֵנוּ
Erets Tsi-yon Y'-ru-sha-la-yim	אֶרֶץ צִיּוֹן יְרוּשָׁלָיִם

As long as a Jewish heart beats, and as long as Jewish eyes look eastward, then our two thousand year hope to be a free nation in Zion is not dead.

LO YISA GOI

Folk   Lyrics: Isaiah

Lo yi-sa goi el goi che-rev
V'lo yil-m'-du od mil-cha-ma

לֹא יִשָּׂא גוֹי אֶל גוֹי חֶרֶב
וְלֹא יִלְמְדוּ עוֹד מִלְחָמָה

Nation shall not lift up sword against nation; neither shall they learn war any more.

YIDDISH

SONGS

OIFN PRIPITCHIK

M. Warshawsky

This song originally titled "Der Alef-Beyz", is so popular that many think of it as a folk song. The music was later used as a theme in the film based on the life of George Gershwin.

Oifn pri-pi-chik brent a fa-ye-rl	אויפן פריפעטשיק ברענט א פייערל
Un in shtub iz hés	און אין שטוב איז הייס
Un der re-be ler-ent klé-ne kin-der-lach	און דער רבי לערנט קליינע קינדערלעך
Dem a-leph béz	דעם אלף-בית
Zét zhe kin-der-lach ge-denkt zhe ta-ye-re	זעט זשע קינדערלעך געדענקט זשע טייערע
Vos ir ler-ent do	וואס איר לערנט דא
Zogt zhe noch a mol un ta-ke noch a mol	זאגט זשע נאך א מאל און טאקע נאך א מאל
Ko-mets a a-leph o	קָמֶץ-אַלֶף אָ
Lernt kin-der mit grois ché-shek	לערנט קינדער מיט גרויס חשק
A-zoi zog ich aich on	אזוי זאג איך אייך אן
Ver s'vet gi-cher fun aich ken-en iv-re	ווער ס'וועט גיכער פון אייך קענען עברי
Der ba-kumt a fon Refrain	דער באקומט א פאן
Az ir vet kinder elter vern	אז איר וועט קינדער עלטער ווערן
Vet ir a-lén far-shtén	וועט איר אליין פארשטיין
Vi fil in di oi-syes li-gn trern	וויפל אין די אותיות ליגן טרערן
Un vi fil ge-vén Refrain	און ווי פיל געוויין
Az ir vet kin-der dem go-les shle-pn	אז איר וועט קינדער דעם גלות שלעפן
Ois-ge-mut-shet zain	אויסגעמוטשעט זיין
Zolt ir fun di oi-syes ko-ach shepn	זאלט איר פון די אותיות כַח שעפן
Kukt in zé a-rain	קוקט אין זיי אריין

A flame burns in the fireplace and the room is warm. The teacher drills the children in the *alef-béz*. When you grow older you will understand that this alphabet contains the tears of our people. When you grow weary you will find comfort in this alphabet

ROZINKES MIT MANDLEN

A. Goldfaden

Abraham Goldfaden known as the "Father of Yiddish Theater" wrote this song in 1880 for his operetta, *Shulamis*. The refrain is an adaptation of a Yiddish folk song, "Unter Yankeles Vigele."

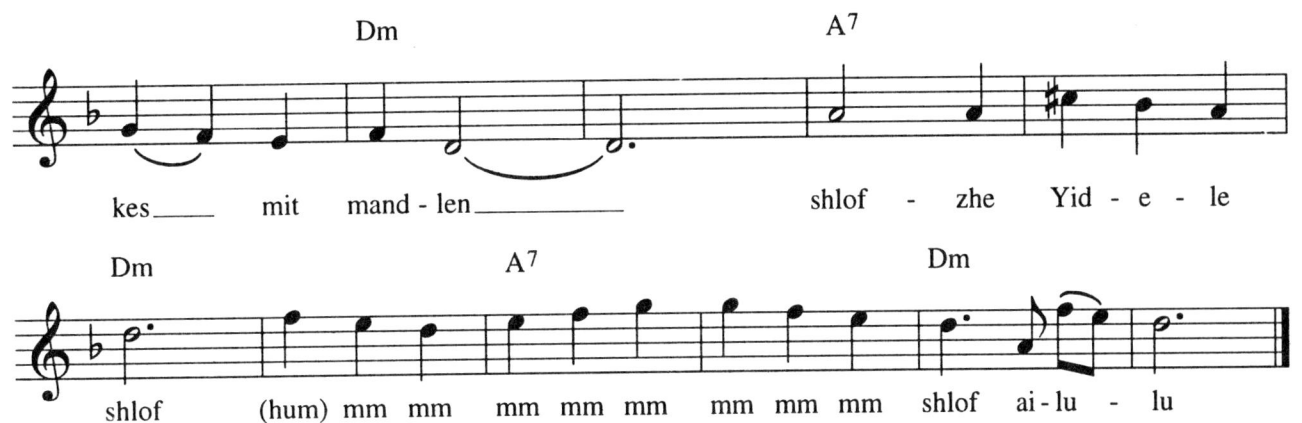

In dem bés-hamik-dosh	אין דעם בית המקדש
In a vin-kl ché-der	אין א ווינקל חדר
Zitst di al-mo-no Bas Tsi-yon a-lén	זיצט די אַלְמָנָה בַת צִיון אליין
Ir ben-yo-chidl Yid-e-le	איהר בֶּן-יָחִיד'ל אידעלע
Vigt zi k'sé-der	וויגט זי כסדר
Un zingt im tsum shlo-fn	און זינגט איהם צום שלאפן
A li-de-le shén	א לידעלע שיין
Ai-lu-lu-lu	אי-לו-לו-לו
Un-ter Yi-de-les vi-gele	אונטער אידעלעס וויגעלע
Shtét a klor-vais tsi-ge-le	שטייט א קלאר ווייס ציגעלע
Dos tsi-ge-le iz ge-forn hand-len	דאס ציגעלע איז געפארן האנדלען
Dos vet zain dain ba-ruf	דאס וועט זיין דיין בארוף
Rozh-in-kes mit mand-len	ראזשינקעס מיט מאנדלען
Shlof zhe Yi-de-le shlof	שלאף זשע אידעלע שלאף

In a corner of the Temple the widowed daughter of Zion sits, rocking her only son, Yidele, to sleep. She sings him a tender lullaby about a snow white kid. The kid has been to market. That will be Yidele's calling too—trading in raisins and almonds.

DER REBE ELIMELECH

M. Nadir

A Yiddish version of the English song, Old *King Cole*.
Poem and music by Moshe Nadir (1885-1943).

Az der Re-be E-li-me-lech	אז דער רבי אלימלך
Iz ge-vorn zé-er fré-lech,	איז געוואָרן זייער פֿריילעך
Is ge-vorn zé-er fré-lech Eli-me-lech	איז געוואָרן זייער פֿריילעך אלימלך
Hot er ois-ge-ton di t'-filn	האָט ער אויסגעטאָן די תפֿילין
Un hot on-ge-ton di bri-ln	און האָט אָנגעטאָן די ברילן
Un ge-shikt noch di fid-lers di tsvé	און געשיקט נאָך די פֿידלערס די צוויי
Un di fidl-di-ke fid-lers	און די פֿידלדיקע פֿידלערס
Hobn fidl-dik ge-fidlt	האָבן פֿידלדיק געפֿידלט
Hobn fidl-dik ge-fidlt hobn zé	האָבן פֿידלדיק געפֿידלט האָבן זיי
Az der Re-be E-li-me-lech	אז דער רבי אלימלך
Iz ge-vorn noch mer fré-lech,	איז געוואָרן נאָך מער פֿריילעך
Is ge-vorn noch mer fré-lech Eli-me-lech	איז געוואָרן נאָך מער פֿריילעך אלימלך
Hot er op-ge-macht hav-do-le	האָט ער אָפּגעמאַכט הַבְדָלָה
Mitn sha-mes Reb Naf-to-le	מיטן שמש ר׳ נפֿתלי
Un ge-shikt noch di paik-lers di tsvé	און געשיקט נאָך די פּייקלערס די צוויי
Un di pai-kel-di-ke paik-lers	און די פּייקעלדיקע פּייקלערס
Hobn pai-kel-dik ge-pai-kelt	האָבן פּייקלדיק געפּייקלט
Hobn pai-kel-dik ge-pai-kelt hobn zé	האָבן פּייקלדיק געפּייקלט האָבן זיי
Az der Re-be E-li-me-lech	אז דער רבי אלימלך
Iz ge-vorn gor shtark fré-lech,	איז געוואָרן גאָר שטאַרק פֿריילעך
Is ge-vorn gor shtark fré-lech Eli-me-lech	איז געוואָרן גאָר שטאַרק פֿריילעך אלימלך
Hot er ois-ge-ton dos ki-tl	האָט ער אויסגעטאָן דאָס קיטל
Un hot on-ge-ton dos hi-tl	און האָט אָנגעטאָן דאָס היטל
Un ge-shikt noch di tsim-blers di tsvé	און געשיקט נאָך די צימבלערס די צוויי
Un di tsim-bl-di-ke tsim-blers	און די צימבלדיקע צימבלערס
Hobn tsim-bl-dik ge-tsim-blt	האָבן צימבלדיק געצימבלט
Hobn tsim-bl-dik ge-tsim-blt hobn zé	האָבן צימבלדיק געצימבלט האָבן זיי

When Rabbi Elimelech became merry he removed his phylacteries, put on his glasses and summoned his two fiddlers. The fiddlers truly fiddled. When he became even merrier he called for his cymbalists and his drummers.

ÉLI ÉLI

J. Sandler

The song, arranged by H. A. Russotto, was published in 1907. It was originally performed by Boris Thomashefsky (of Yiddish Theater fame). Many singers since then, among them Cantor Yossele Rosenblatt and Al Jolson, have included the song in their repertoires and recordings.

Eli Eli lo-mo a-zav-to-ni?
In fa-yer un flam hot men undz ge-brent
I-ber-al ge-macht undz tsu shand un tsu shpot
Doch op-tsu-ven-den hot undz ké-ner nisht ge-kent
Fun dir main Got un fun dain hé-lig-er To-ro
Fun dain ge-bot
Eli Eli lo-mo a-zav-to-ni?
Tog un nacht nor ich tracht
Fun dir main Got
Ich hit mit mo-ro op dain To-ro
Un dain ge-bot
Re-te mich re-te mich fun ge-far
Vi a mol di o-vos fun bé-zn g'-zar
Her main ge-bét un main ge-vén
Hel-fn ken-stu doch nor a-lén
Sh'-ma Yis-ro-él A-do-noi E-lo-hé-nu
A-do-noi e-chod

אֵלִי אֵלִי לָמָה עֲזַבְתָּנִי
אין פייער און פלאם האט מען אונז געברענט
איבעראל געמאכט אונז צו שאנד און צו שפאט
דאך אפצו-ווענדען האט אונז קיינער ניט געקענט
פון דיר מיין גאט מיט דיין היילינער תורה
פון דיין געבאט
אֵלִי אֵלִי לָמָה עֲזַבְתָּנִי
טאג און נאכט נאר איך טראכט
פון דיר מיין גאט
איך היט מיט מורא אפ דיין תּוֹרָה
און דיין געבאט
רעטע מיך אוי רעטע מיך פון געפאר
ווי א מאל די אָבות פון בייזן גְזַר
הער מיין געבעט און מיין געווען
העלפען קענסטו דאך נאר אליין
שְׁמַע יִשְׂרָאֵל יְיָ אֱלֹהֵינוּ
יְיָ אֶחָד

My God, why have you forsaken me? They burned us in fire and flames. Everywhere they shamed and mocked us. No one could turn us away from you, your holy Tora and commandment.

UN AZ DER REBE ZINGT

Folktune

Un az der re-be zingt
Zing-en a-le cha-si-dim

Un az der re-be tantst
Tan-tsen a-le cha-si-dim

Un az der re-be lacht
La-chen a-le cha-si-dim

Un az der re-be shloft
Shlof-en a-le cha-si-dim

און אז דער רבי זינגט
זינגען אלע חסידים

און אז דער רבי טאנצט
טאנצען אלע חסידים

און אז דער רבי לאכט
לאכען אלע חסידים

און אז דער רבי שלאפט
שלאפן אלע חסידים

When the Rebbe sings all the chassidim sing and when he dances all the chassidim dance. When the rebbe laughs the chassidim laugh and when he sleeps they also sleep.

BAI MIR BISTU SHÉN

Music: S. Secunda   Lyrics: J. Jacobs

Surely one of the most popular of all Yiddish-American songs of the twentieth century, *Bai Mir Bistu Shen*, was sold by its composer, Sholom Secunda, during the early part of the twentieth century. Fifty years later the copyright reverted back to the composer while he was still alive. Both Yiddish and English versions of the song were performed and recorded by outstanding artists throughout the world.

81

Ven du zolst zain shvarts vi a tu-ter	ווען דו זאלסט זיין שווארץ ווי א טאטער
Ven du host oi-gen vi a ku-ter	ווען די האסט אויגען ווי א קאטער
Un ven du hinkst tsu-bis-lach	און ווען דו הינקסט צוביסלאך
Host hil-tser-ne fis-lach	האסט הילצערנע פיסלאך
Zog ich dos art mich nit	זאג איך דאס ארט מיך ניט
Un ven du host a nar-ish-en shmé-chel	און ווען דו האסט א נארישען שמייכעל
Un ven du host Vai-zo-so's sé-chel	און ווען דו האסט ויזתה'ס שֵׂכֶל
Ven du bist vild vi a In-di-a-ner	ווען דו ביסט ווילד ווי א אינדיאנער
Bist a-fi-lu a Ga-lits-ya-ner	ביזט אפילו א גאליציאנער
Zog ich dos art mich nit	זאג איך דאס ארט מיך ניט
Zog mir vi er-klers-tu dos?	זאג מיר ווי ערקלערסטו דאס?
'Ch-vel dir zog-en shoin far-vos	כ'וועל דיר זאגען שוין פארוואס
Vail bai mir bis-tu shén	ווייל ביי מיר ביסטו שעהן
Bai mir hos-tu chén	ביי מיר האָסטו חֵן
Bai mir bis-tu	ביי מיר ביסטו
E-ner oif der velt	איינער אויף דער וועלט
Bai mir bis-tu git	ביי מיר ביסטו גיט
Bai mir hos-tu "it"	ביי מיר האסטו "איט"
Bai mir bis-tu ta-yer-er fun gelt	ביי מיר ביסטו טייערער פון געלט
Fil shé-ne méd-lach hob-en	פיל שעהנע מיידלאך האבען
Shoin ge-volt nem-en mich	שוין געוואלט נעמען מיך
Un fun zé a-le ois-ge-klib-en	און פון זיי אלע אויסגעקליבען
Hob ich nor dich	האב איך נאר דיך
Vail bai mir bis-tu shén	ביי מיר ביסטו שעהן
Bai mir hos-tu chén	ביי מיר האָסטו חֵן
Bai mir bis-tu	ביי מיר ביסטו
E-ner oif der velt	איינער אויף דער וועלט

To me you are the most beautiful of all the young ladies. Many girls have been interested in me but from all of them I have chosen you.

ÉSHES CHAYIL

Music: J. Rumshinsky   Lyrics: I. Lillian

©by J.J. Kammen Music

An e-me-se é-shes cha-yil	אן אֱמֶתִּיע אֵשֶׁת חַיִל
A ta-ye-re kain tra-ye-re	א טייערע קיין טרייערע
Fun dir 'z nit do	פון דיר ז׳ניטא
A gol-de-ne n'-sho-mo	א גאָלדענע נְשָׁמָה
A na-chas a n'-cho-mo	א נַחַת א נְחָמָה
A li-be froi a gu-te ma-men-yu	א ליבע פרוי א גוטע מאמעניו
A-za froi vi zi	אזא פיינע פרוי ווי זי
Brengt in hoiz nor har-mo-ni	ברענגט אין הויז נאר האַרמאָני
S'lé-ben iz a sym-pho-ny	ס׳לעבען איז א סימפאָני
É-she cha-yil mi yim-tso	אֵשֶׁת חַיִל מִי יִמְצָא

A true woman of valor-a loving wife and a good mother. Such a woman brings harmony into the home and life becomes a symphony.

A YIDISHE MAME

J. Yellen & L. Pollack

Possibly the all-time favorite song dedicated to the Jewish mother. The song is found in the repertoire of most singers of Yiddish music from 1925 on.

85

Ich vil bai aich a ka-she fré-gen	איך ווילביי אייך א קאשיא פרעגן
Zogt mir ver es ken	זאגט מיר ווער עס קען
Mit vel-che ta-ye-re far-me-gens	מיט וועלכע טאיערע פערמעגנס
Bentsht Got a-le-men	בענטשט גאט אלעמען
Men koift es nit far ké-ne gelt	מען קויפט עס ניט פאר קיינע געלט
Dos git men nor um-zist	דאס גיט מען נאר אומזיסט
Un doch az men far-lirt dos	און דאך אז מען פארלירט דאס
Vi fil tre-ren men far-gist	ווי פיהל טרערן מען פארגיסט
A tsvé-te git men ké-nem nit	א צווייטע גיט מען קיינעם ניט
Es helft nit kain ge-vén	עס העלפט ניט קיין געוויין
Oi ver es hot far-loi-ren	אוי ווער עס האט פארלוירן
Der vés shoin vos ich mén	דער ווייס שוין וואס איך מיין
A yi-di-she ma-me	א אידישע מאמע
Es gibt nit be-ser in der velt	עס גיבט ניט בעסער אין דער וועלט
A yi-di-she ma-me	א אידישע מאמע
Oi vé vi bi-ter ven zi félt	אוי ווי ווי ביטער ווען זי פעהלט
Vi shén un lich-tig iz in hoiz	ווי שיין אונד ליכטיג איז אין הויז
Ven di ma-me 'z do	ווען די מאמע'ז דא
Vi troi-rig fin-ster vert	ווי טרויריג פינסטער ווערט
Ven Got nemt ir oif o-lom ha-bo	ווען גאט נעמט איהר אויף עוֹלָם הַבָּא
In vas-er un fa-yer	אין וואסער אונד פייער
Volt zi ge-lof-en far ir kind	וואלט זי געלאפן פאר איהר קינד
Nit halt-en ir ta-yer	ניט האלטן איהר טייער
Dos iz ge-vis di gres-te zind	דאס איז געוויס די גרעסטע זינד
Oi vi glik-lich und raich	אוי ווי גליקליך אונד רייך
Iz der mentsh vos hot	איז דער מענטש וואס האט
A za shé-ne ma-to-ne ge-shenkt fun Got	א זא שיינע מתנה געשענקט פון גאט
Nor ain alt-itsh-ke Yi-di-she ma-me	נאר איין אלטיטשקע אידישע מאמע
Ma-me main	מאמע מיין

My Yidishe ma-me I need her more than ever now
My Yidishe ma-me I'd like to kiss her wrinkled brow
I long to hold her hand once more as in days gone by
And ask her to forgive me for things I did that made her cry
How few were her pleasures, she never cared for fashion styles
Her jewels and her treasures she found in her baby's smiles
O I know that I owe what I am today
To that dear little lady who's young yet gray
To that wonderful Yidishe ma-me
Ma-me mine.

PAPIROSN

H. Yablokoff

Popular song written by, Herman Yablokoff (1903-1981) As a child during World War I he peddled cigarettes. In 1932, he introduced part of the song at the end of a program on radio station WEVD in New York City. *Papirosn* became an instant hit and thousands of copies of the song sheet were printed. *Papirosn* became very popular in Europe as well.

A kal-te nacht a ne-bel-di-ge	א קאלטע נאכט א נעבעלדיגע
Fins-ter u-me-tum	פינסטער אומעטום
Shtét a yin-ge-le frar-troi-ert	שטייט א אינגעלע פארטרויערט
Un kukt zich a-rum	און קוקט זיך ארום
Fun ré-gn shtitst im nor a vant	פון רעגן שיצט אים נאר א וואנט
A ko-shi-kl halt er in hant	א קאשיקל האלט ער אין האנט
Un zai-ne oi-gen be-tn yé-dn shtum	און זיינע אויגן בעטן יעדן שטום
Ich hob shoin nisht kain ko-ach mer	איך האב שוין ניט קיין כח מער
A-rum-tsu-gén in gas	ארומצוגיין אין גאס
Hun-ge-rik un op-ge-ri-sn	הונגעריק און אפגעריסן
Fun dem re-gn nas	פון דעם רעגן נאס
Ich shlep a-rum zich fun ba-ni-gen	איך שלעפ ארום זיך פון באניגען
Ké-ner git nit tsu far-di-nen	קיינער גיט ניט צו פארדינען
A-le la-chn ma-chn fun mir shpas	אלע לאכן מאכן פון מיר שפאס
Ku-pit-ye koift- zhe koift-zhe pa-pi-ro-sn	קופיטיע קויפט זשע קויפט זשע פאפיראסן
Tru-ke-ne fun re-gn nit far-go-sn	טרוקענע פון רעגן ניט פארגאסן
Koift- zhe bil-ik b'-ne-mo-nes	קויפט זשע ביליק בנאמנות
Koift un hot oif mir rach-mo-nes	קויפט און האט אויף מיר רחמנות
Ra-te-vet fun hun-ger mich a-tsind	ראטעוועט פון הונגער מיך אצינד
Ku-pit-ye koift- zhe shvé-ba-lach an-ti-kn	קופיטיע קויפט זשע שוועבאלאך אנטיקן
Der mit vet ir a yo-siml der-kvi kn	דער מיט וועט איר א יתומ'ל דערקוויקן
Um-zist main shrai-en un main loi-fn	אומזיסט מיין שרייען און מיין לויפן
Ké-ner vil bai mir nit koi-fn	קיינער וויל ביי מיר ניט קויפן
Ois-gén vel ich mu-zn vi a hunt	אויסגיין וועל איך מוזן ווי א הונט

On a cold, misty night a hungry little boy tries to sell cigarettes. "Buy from me," he cries "save me from starvation."

YANKELE

M. Gebirtig

This lullaby was written by Mordechai Gebirtig (1877-1942), one of the last popular Yiddish folk poets. Gebirtig's songs became immediate hits in the 1920's. They were sung on both sides of the Atlantic, due largely to their popularization by celebrities of the Yiddish theatre.

Shlof zhe mir shoin Yankele main shé-ner	שלאָף-זשע מיר שוין יאַנקעלע מיין שיינער
Di é-gel-ech di shvarts-in-ke mach tsu	די אייגעלאַך די שוואַרצינקע מאַך צו
A yin-ge-le vos hot shoin a-le tsén-de-lach	אַ ייִנגעלע וואָס האָט שוין אַלע ציינדלאַך
Muz noch di ma-me zing-en ai-lu-lu	מוז נאָך די מאַמע זינגען איי-ליו-ליו
A yin-ge-le vos hot shoin a-le tsén-de-lach	אַ ייִנגעלע וואָס האָט שוין אַלע ציינדלאַך
Un vet mit ma-zl bald in ché-der gén	און וועט מיט מזל באַלד אין חדר גיין
Un lern-en vet er chu-mosh un ge-mo-ro	און לערנען וועט ער חומש און גמרא
Zol vén-en ven di ma-me vigt im ain?	זאָל וויינען ווען די מאַמע וויגט אים איין?
A yin-ge-le vos lern-en vet ge-mo-ro	אַ ייִנגעלע וואָס לערנען וועט גמרא
Ot shtét der ta-te kvelt un hert zich tsu	אָט שטייט דער טאַטע קוועלט און הערט זיך צו
A yin-ge-le vos vakst a tal-mid-cho-chom	אַ ייִנגעלע וואָס וואַקסט אַ תלמיד חכם
Lozt gan-tse necht der ma-men nisht tsu-ru?	לאָזט גאַנצע נעכט דער מאַמען נישט צורו?
A yin-ge-le vos vakst a tal-mid-cho-chom	אַ ייִנגעלע וואָס וואַקסט אַ תלמיד חכם
Un a ge-ni-ter so-cher oich tsu glaich	און אַ געניטער סוחר אויך צוגלייך
A yin-ge-le a klu-ger cho-sn-bo-cher	אַ ייִנגעלע אַ קלוגער חתן בחור
Zol li-gen a-zoi nas vi in a taich?	זאָל ליגן אַזוי נאַס ווי אין אַ טייך?
Nu shlof-zhe mir main klu-ger chosn-bocher	נו שלאָף-זשע מיר מיין קלוגער חתן בחור
Der-vail lig-stu in vi-gele bai mir	דערווייל ליגסטו אין וויגעלע ביי מיר
S'vet kost-en noch fil mi un ma-mes tre-ren	ס'וועט קאָסטען נאָך פיל מי און מאַמעס טרערן
Biz ven es s'vet a mentsh a-rois fun dir	ביז ווען ס'וועט אַ מענטש אַרויס פון דיר

Sleep my beautiful Yankele, close your beautiful dark eyes. Why is it that a young fellow with all his teeth in place still needs his mother to sing him to sleep.

DI GRINE KUZINE

This song was one of the most popular songs of immigrant life in America.

A. Schwartz   Lyrics: H. Prizant

©by J.J. Kammen Music

Es iz tsu mir iz ge-kum-en a ku-zi-ne
Shén vi gold iz zi ge-ven di gri-ne
Be-ke-lach vi roi-te po-me-rants-en
Fi-se-lach vos be-ten zich tsum tan-tsen

Her-a-lach gold-e-ne ge-lag-te
Tsén-de-lach vi pe-re-lach ge-tag-te
E-ge-lach vi tai-be-lach a tsvil-ing
Lip-e-lach vi kar-she-lach in fri-ling

עס איז צו מיר געקומען א קוזינע
שעהן ווי גאלד איז זי געווען די גרינע
בעקעלאך ווי רויטע פאמעראנצען
פיסעלאך וואס בעטען זיך צום טאנצען

הערעלאך גאלדענע געלאגטע
צײנדעלאך ווי פערעלאך געטאגטע
אײגעלאך ווי טײבעלאך א צווילינג
ליפעלאך ווי קארשעלאך אין פרילינג

A pretty cousin came to me from Europe. Her cheeks were like red oranges, her feet just begging to dance. She had beautiful golden hair and teeth white like pearls. She was a true beauty.

M'CHUTENESTE MAINE

Folk song, text and music published in 1938 by M. Beregovski and I. Feller.

Folktune

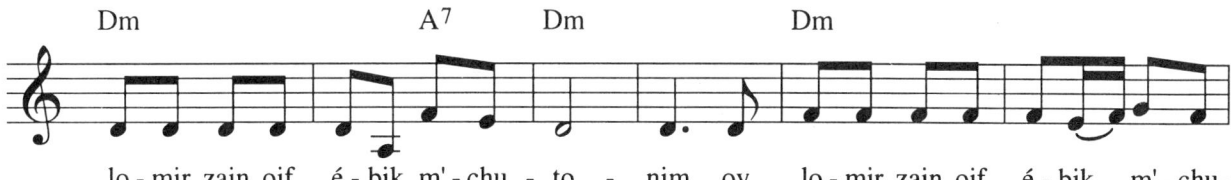

M'-chu-tén-is-te mai-ne	מחותנתטע מיינע
M'-chu-tén-es-te ge-tra-ye	מחותנתטע געטרייע
Oy lo-mir zain	אוי לאמיר זיין
Oif é-bik m-'chu-to-nim	אויף אייביק מחותנים
Ich gib aich a-vek	איך גיב אייך אוועק
Main toch-ter far a shnur	מיין טאכטער פאר א שנור
Zi zol bai aich	זי זאל ביי אייך
Nit on-ver-en dos po-nim	ניט אנווערן דאס פנים

My dear m'chuténiste, let us always be good in-laws. I am giving you my daughter as a daughter-in-law. May she always be treated with love.

TUMBALALAIKA

Folksong

This very popular song was first published in the United States in 1940. It has been recorded by many Yiddish singers since that time. Lyrics other than the ones presented here have also appeared. These however, are the most often used lyrics.

Shtét a bo-cher un er tracht	שטייט א בחור און ער טראכט
Tracht un tracht a gan-tse nacht	טראכט און טראכט א גאנצע נאכט
Vé-men tsu ne-men un nisht far-she-men	וועמען צו נעמען און נישט פארשעמען
Ve-men tsu ne-men un nisht far-she-men	וועמען צו נעמען און נישט פארשעמען
Tum-bala tum-bala tum-balalaika	טום-באלא טום-באלא טום-באלאלייקע
Tum-bala tum-bala tum-balalaika	טום-באלא טום-באלא טום-באלאלייקע
Tum-balalaika shpil balalaika	טום-באלאלייקע שפיל באלאלייקע
Shpil balalaika fré-lech zol zain!	שפיל באלאלייקע פריילעך זאל זיין
Mé-dl mé-dl ch'vil bai dir fré-gn	מיידל, מיידל כ׳ווילביי דיר פרעגן
Vos ken vak-sn vak-sn on ré-gn?	וואס קען וואקסן, וואקסן אן רעגן
Vos ken bren-en un nisht oyf-hern?	וואס קען ברענען און נישט אויפהערן
Vos ken benk-en vé-nen on trern? *Refrain:*	וואס קען בענקען וויינען אן טרערן
Nar-ish-er bo-cher vos darf-stu fré-gn?	נארישער בחור וואס דארפסטו פרעגן
A shtén ken vak-sn vak-sn on ré-gn	א שטיין קען וואקסן, וואקסן אן רעגן
Li-be ken brene-n un nisht oif-hern	ליבע קען ברענען און נישט אויפהערן
A harts ken benk-en vé-nen on trern *Refrain:*	א הארץ קען בענקען וויינען אן טרערן

All night long a young man worries which girl to marry without embarrasing another one. "Young lady can you tell me what grows without rain, what yearns without tears, what can burn forever?" "Silly lad, a stone can grow without rain, a heart can yearn without tears and love can burn forever."

A BRIVELE DER MAMEN

S. Shmulewitz

A Brivele Der Mamen was one of the most beloved songs of the immigration era on both sides of the Atlantic.

Main kind, main trést, du forst a-vek,	מיין קינד מיין טרייסט דו פארסט אוועק
Zé zai a zun a gut-er,	זע זיי א זון א גוטער
Dich bét mit tre-rn un mit shrek	דיך בעט מיט טרערן און מיט שרעק
Dain tra-ye li-be mu-ter	דיין טרייע ליבע מוטער
Di forst main kind main én-tsik kind	דו פארסט מיין קינד מיין איינציק קינד
A-ri-ber vai-te ya-men	אריבער ווייטע ימען
Ach kum a-hin nor frish ge-zunt	אך קום אהין נאר פריש געזונט
Un nit far-ges dain ma-men	און ניט פארגעס דיין מאמען
Yo for ge-zunt un kum mit glik	יא פאר געזונט און קום מיט גליק
Zé yé-de voch a bri-vl shik	זע יעדע וואך א בריוול שיק
Dain ma-mes harts main kind der-kvik	דיין מאמעס הארץ מיין קינד דערקוויק
A bri-vele der ma-men	א בריוועלע דער מאמען
Zol-stu nit far-za-men	זאלסטו ניט פארזאמען
Shraib ge-shvind li-bes kind	שרייב געשווינד ליבעס קינד
Shenk ir di n'-cho-mo	שענק איר די נחמה
Di ma-me vet dain bri-ve-le lé-zn	די מאמע וועט דיין בריוועלע לעזן
Un zi vet ge-ni-zn	און זי וועט גענעזן
Hélst ir shmarts ir bi-ter harts,	היילסט איר שמארץ איר ביטער הארץ
Der-kvikst ir di n'-sh-omo	דערקוויקט איר די נשמה

My child you are leaving for a land far across the seas. Remember to send a letter each week to a lonely mother.

BELZ

Music: A. Olshanetsky Lyrics: J. Jacobs

One of the most popular Yiddish theatre songs that expressed longing for hometowns in Eastern Europe. Belz was written for Alexander Olshanetsky's play *The Song of the Ghetto*.

©by J.J. Kammen Music

Belz main shté-te-le Belz	בעלז-מיין שטעטעלע בעלז
Main hé-me-le vu ich hob	מיין היימעלע וו איך האב
Mai-ne kinder-she yorn far-bracht	מיינע קינדערשע יארן פארבראכט
Zait ir a mol geven in Belz,	זייט איר א מאל געווען אין
Main shté-tele Belz	בעלז-מיין שטעטעלע בעלז
In o-re-men shti-be-le	אין ארעמען שטיבעלע
Mit ale kin-der-lech dort ge-lacht	מיט אלע קינדערלעך דארט געלאכט
Yé-dn Sha-bos flég ich loi-fn	יעדן שבת פלעג איך לויפן
Dort mit der tchi-na glaich	דארט מיט דער תְחִינָה גלייך
Tsu zit-sn un-ter dem gri-nem bé-me-le	צו זיצן אונטער דעם גרינעם ביימעלע
Lé-nen bai dem taich	לייענען ביי דעם טייך
Belz main shté-te-le Belz	בעלז-מיין שטעטעלע בעלז
Main hé-me-le vu ch'-hob ge-hat	מיין היימעלע וו איך האב געהאט
Di shé-ne cha-lo-mes a sach	די שיינע חלומות א סך

Belz, my little town, the home where I spent my childhood years. Every Sabbath I would run down to read by the river. Belz, my little town where I had so many wonderful dreams.

RÉZELE

M. Gebirtig

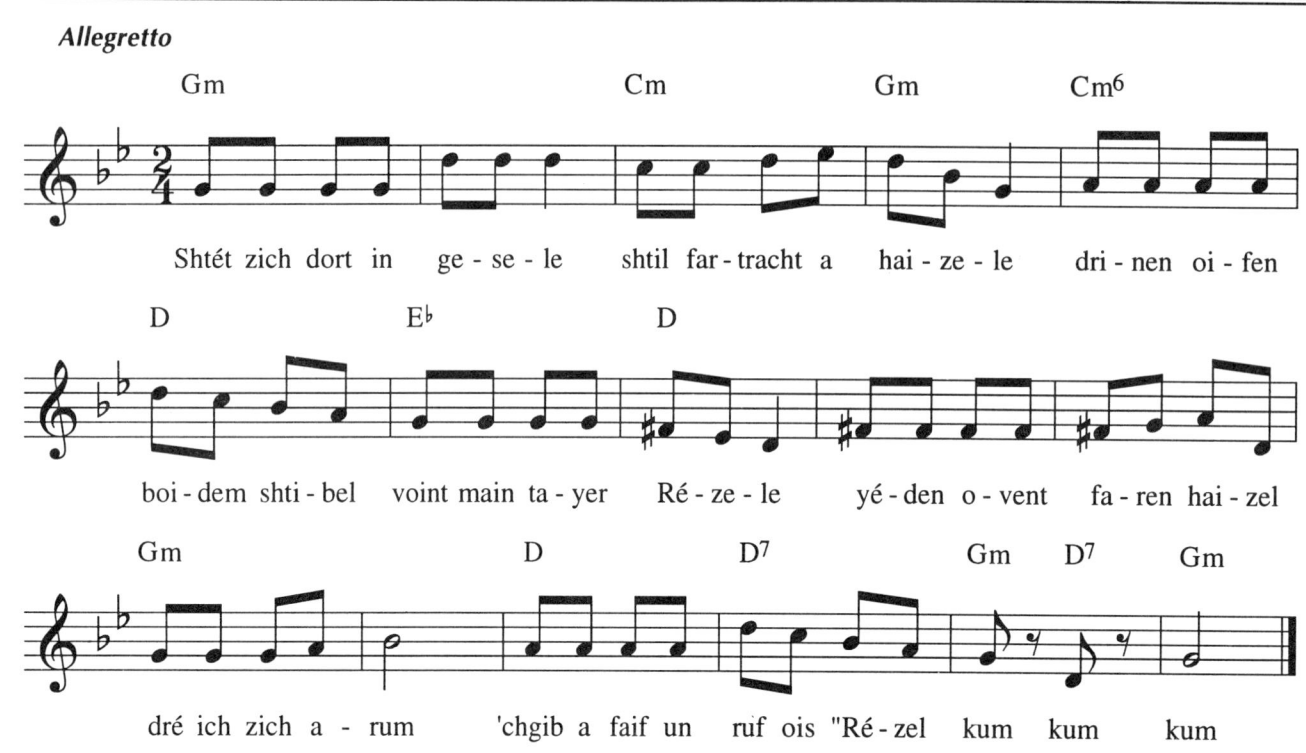

Shtét zich dort in ge-se-le	שטייט זיך דארט אין געסעלע
Shtil far-tracht a hai-ze-le	שטיל פארטראכט א הייזעלע
Drin-en oif-n boi-dem shti-bel	דרינען אויפן בוידעם שטיבל
Voint main ta-yer Rézele	וווינט מיין טייער רייזעלע
Dré ich zich a-rum	דריי איך זיך ארום
'Ch-gib a faif un ruf ois: Rézel	כ'גיב א פייף און רוף אויס: רייזל
Kum kum kum	קום קום קום
Ef-ent zich a fens-ter-l	עפענט זיך א פענצטערל
Vacht oif 's-al-te hai-ze-le	וואכט אויף ס'אלטע הייזעלע
Un bald klingt in shtil-n ge-sl	און באלד קלינגט אין שטילן געסל
A zis kol 's redt Rézele	א זיס קול ס'רעדט רייזעלע
Noch a vai-le vart main lib-er	נאך א ווייילע ווארט מיין ליבער
Bald vel ich zain frai	באלד וועל איך זיין פריי
Gé zich noch a por mol i-ber	גיי זיך נאך א פאר מאל איבער
Éns tsvé drai	איינס צווי דריי

In the attic of a small house lives my dear Rézele. Every evening I pass by and call her to come out. Rézele answers sweetly: "Wait, my dear, I will be ready soon."

YOME YOME

This Yiddish courtship song features a dialogue between a *shadchen* (matchmaker) and a young girl. After offering her a choice of bridegrooms, she is willing to accepts only the young scholar.

Yo-me Yo-me shpil mir a li-de-le
Vos dos mé-de-le vil
Dos mé-de-le vil a por shi-che-lech ho-ben
Muz men gén dem shus-ter zo-gen
Nén ma-me-shi nén
Du kenst mich nit far-shtén
Du vést nit vos ich mén

Yo-me Yo-me shpil mir a li-de-le
Vos dos mé-de-le vil
Dos mé-de-le vil a cho-son-del ho-ben
Darf men gén a shad-chn zo-gen
Yo ma-me-shi yo
Du kenst mich shoin far-shtén
Du vést shoin vos ich mén

יאמע יאמע זינג מיר א לידעלע
וואס דאס מיידעלע וויל
דאס מיידעלע וויל א פאר שיכעלאך האבען
דארף מען געהן דעם שוסטער זאגען
ניין מאמעשו ניין
דו קענסט מיך ניט פארשטעהן
דו ווייסט ניט וואס איך מיין

יאמע יאמע זינג מיר א לידעלע
וואס דאס מיידעלע וויל
דאס מיידעלע וויל א חתנ'ידעל האבען
דארף מען געהן דעם שדכן זאגען
יא מאמעשי יא
דו קענסט מיך שוין פארשטעהן
דו ווייסט שוין וואס איך מיין

Yome, Yome, sing me a little song and tell me exactly what it is
that you want.

SHÉN VI DI L'VONE

Music: J. Rumshinsky   Lyrics: C. Tauber

Menashe Skulnick, the famed comedic Yiddish actor used to say that this song was especially written for him. He stopped performing the song when it became a big hit and was sung by many other Yiddish singers.

Shén vi di l'-vo-ne lech-tig vi di shte-rn fun hi-ml a ma-to-ne bis-tu mir tzu-ge-shikt Main glick hob ich ge-vun-en ven ich hob dich ge-fun-en du shainst vi toi-znt zun-en host main harts ba-glikt Dai-ne tsén-de-lach vai-se pe-re-lach mit dai-ne shé-ne oi-gn dai-ne chén-de-lach dai-ne he-re-lach host mich tsu-ge-tsoi-gn shén vi di l'-vo-ne lich-tig vi di shte-rn fun hi-ml a ma-to-ne hos-tu mich tsu-ge-shikt

©by J.J. Kammen Music

Shén vi di l'-vo-ne	שײן װי די לבנה
Lech-tig vi di shte-ren	לעכטיג װי די שטערן
Fun hi-ml a ma-to-ne	פון הימל א מתנה
Bis-tu mir tsu-ge-shikt	ביסטו מיר צוגעשיקט
Main glik hob ich ge-vun-en	מײן גליק האב איך געװאונען
Ven ich hob dich ge-fun-en	װען איך האב דיך געפונען
Di shainst vi toi-zent zun-en	די שײנסט װי טױזנט זונען
Du host main hartz ba-glikt	דו האסט מײן הארץ באגליקט
Dai-ne tsén-da-lach vai-se pe-re-lach	דײנע צײנדאלעך װײסע פערעלעך
Mit dai-ne shé-ne oi-gen	מיט דײנע שײנע אױגן
Dai-ne chén-de-lech dai-ne her-a-lech	דײנע חנדעלעך דײנע הערעלעך
Host mich tsu-ge-tsoi-gen	האסט מיך צוגעצױגן
Shén vi di l'-vo-ne	שײן װי די לבנה
Lech-tig vi di shte-rn	לעכטיג װי די שטערן
Fun hi-ml a ma-to-ne	פון הימל א מתנה
Bis-tu mir tsu-ge-shikt	ביסטו מיר צוגעשיקט

Pretty as the moon, bright as the stars, you are a heaven-sent gift to me.

VI AHIN ZOL ICH GÉN

Music: O. Strock   Lyrics: S. Korn-Teuer

Written before World War II, **Vu Ahin Zol Ich Gen** was popular in the ghettos and D.P. camps. The lyrics are attributed to S. Korntayer, a Yiddish actor who died in the Warsaw ghetto in 1942.

Der Yid vert ge-yogt un ge-plogt
Nisht zi-cher iz far im yéder tog
Zain le-bn iz a fins-te-re nacht
Kain shtré-bn alts far im iz far-macht
Far-lo-zn bloiz mit son-im kain fraint
Kain hof-nung on a zi-che-rn haint
Vi a-hin zol ich gén
Ver kon ent-fern mir
Vi a-hin zol ich gén
Az far-shlo-sn iz yéde tir
'Siz di velt grois ge-nug
Nor far mir iz eng un klén
Vi a blik 'ch-muz tsu-rik
'S-iz tsu-shtert yé-de brik
Vi a-hin zol ich gén

דער איד ווערט געיאגט און געפלאגט
נישט זיכער איז פאר אים יעדער טאג
זיין לעבן איז א פינסטערע נאכט
קיין שטרעבן אלץ פאר אים איז פארמאכט
פארלאזן בלויז מיט שונאים קיין פריינט
קיין האפנונג אן א זיכערן היינט
ווי אהין זאל איך גיין?
ווער קאן ענטפערן מיר
ווי אהין זאל איך גיין
אז פארשלאסן איז יעדע טיר
ס'איז די וועלט גרויס גענוג
נאר פאר מיר איז ענג און קליין
ווי א בליק כ'מוז צוריק
ס'איז צושטערט יעדע בריק
ווי אהין זאל איך גיין

Singable English
Tell me where can I go, there's no place I can see
Where to go, where to go, every door is closed to me
To the left to the right, it's the same in every land
There's nowhere to go, and it's me who should know
Wont you please understand
Now I know where to go, where my folks proudly stand
Let me go, let me go, to that precious promised land
No more left, no more right, lift your head for there is light
I am proud can't you see for at last I am free
No more wandering for me!

S'BRENT

M. Gebirtig

Mordechai Gebirtig wrote this stirring song following a 1938 progrom in Poland. It was sung in the ghettos and has become one of the most often performed commemorative songs.

S'brent bri-der-lech s'brent
Oi und-zer o-rem shte-tl ne-bech brent
Bé-ze vin-tn mkit yir-go-zun
Rai-sn bre-chn un tsu-blo-zn
Shtar-ker noch di vil-de flam-en
Alts a-rum shoin brent
Un ir shtét un kukt a-zoi zich
Mit far-lég-te hent
Un ir shtét un kukt a-zoi zich
Und-zer shte-tl brent!

ס׳ברענט ברידעלעך ס׳ברענט
אוי אונדזער ארעם שטעטל נעבעך ברענט
בײזע ווינטן מיט ירגזון
רײסן ברעכן און צעבלאזן
שטארקער נאך די ווילדע פלאמען
אלץ ארום שוין ברענט
און איר שטײט און קוקט אזוי זיך
מיט פארלייגטע הענט
און איר שטײט און קוקט אזוי זיך
אונדזער שטעטל ברענט!

It is burning dear brothers, it is burning! Our poor little town is burning! Angry winds whip the flames. Everything is on fire! And you stand helplessly and stare while the flames grow higher and our little town burns.

ZOG NIT KÉNMOL

Folk

Zog Nit Kenmol became the hymn of the United Partisan Organization in 1943. It spread to all the concentration camps in Eastern Europe and later to Jewish communities the world over. It was translated into several languages. Today, along with *Ani Ma'amin* it is sung at memorial meetings for martyred Jews.

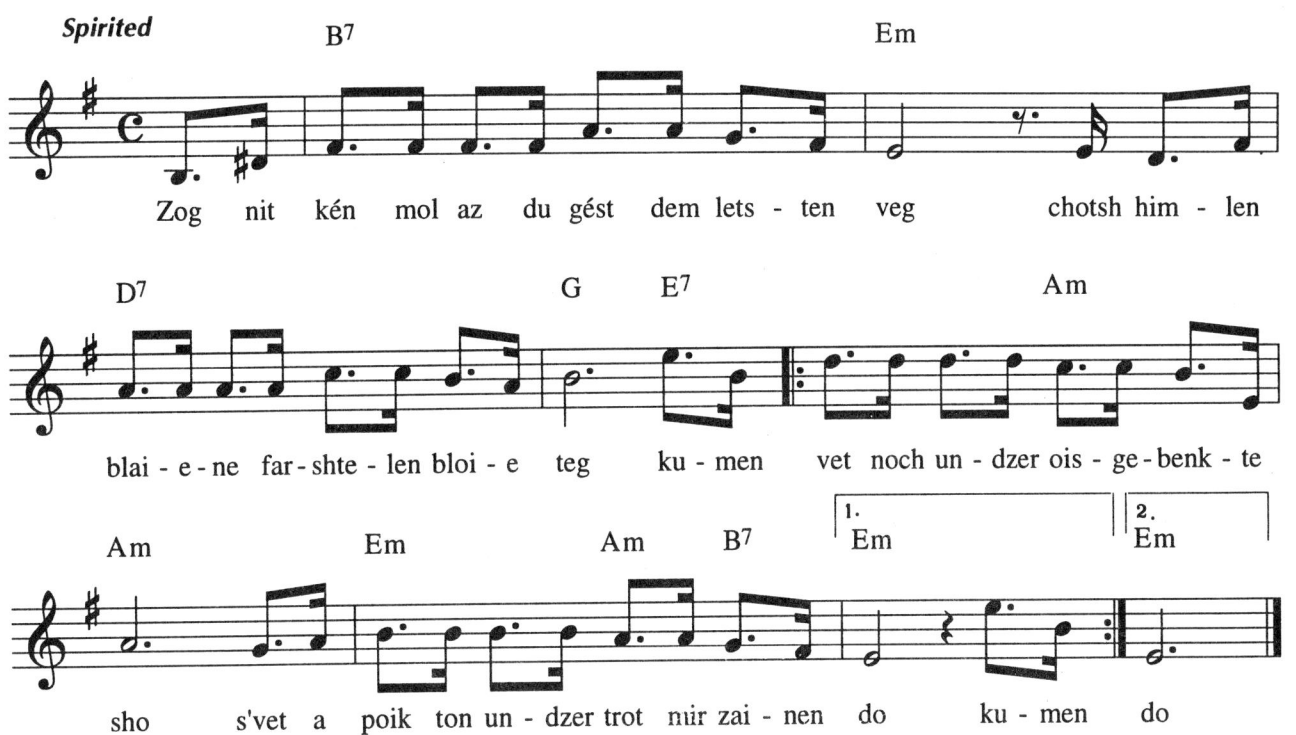

Zog nit kén-mol az du gést dem lets-tn veg
Chotsh him-len bla-ye-ne far-shte-ln blo-ye teg
Ku-men vet noch un-dzer ois-ge-benk-te sho
S'vet a poik ton und-zer trot— mir zain-en do!

זאָג ניט קיין מאָל אַז דו גייסט דעם לעצטן וועג
כאָטש הימלען בלייענע פֿאַרשטעלן בלויע טעג
קומען וועט נאָך אונדזער אויסגעבענקטע שעה
ס׳וועט אַ פּויק טאָן אונדזער טראָט -מיר זיינען דאָ!

Fun grin-empal-men-land biz vaisn land fun shné
Mir ku-men on mit und-zer pain mit und-zer vé
Un vu ge-fa-ln s'iz a shprits fun und-zer blut
Shpro-tsn vet dort und-zer g'-vu-ro und-zer mut

פֿון גרינעם פּאַלמענלאַנד ביז װײַסן לאַנד פֿון שניי
מיר קומען אָן מיט אונדזער פּיין מיט אונדזער וויי
און װוּ געפֿאַלן ס׳איז אַ שפּריץ פֿון אונדזער בלוט
שפּראָצן וועט דאָרט אונדזער גבֿורה אונדזער מוט

S-'vet di mor-gn zun ba-gil-dn undz dem haint
Un der nech-tn vet far-shvin-dn mi-tn faind
Nor oib far-zam-en vet di zun in dem ka-yor
Vi a pa-rol zol gén dos lid fun dor tsu dor

ס׳וועט די מאָרגן זון באַגילדן אונדז דעם היינט
און דער נעכטן וועט פֿאַרשווינדן מיטן פֿײַנד
נאָר אויב פֿאַרזאַמען וועט די זון אין דעם קאַיאָר-
ווי אַ פּאַראָל זאָל גיין דאָס ליד פֿון דור צו דור

Dos lid ge-shri-bn iz mit blut un nit mit blai
S'iz nit kén li-dl fun a foi-gl oif der frai
Dos hot a folk tsvi-shn faln-di-ke vent
Dos lid ge-zung-en mit na-gan-es in di hent!

דאָס ליד געשריבן איז מיט בלוט און ניט מיט בליי
ס׳איז ניט קיין לידל פֿון אַ פֿויגל אויף דער פֿריי
דאָס האָט אַ פֿאָלק צווישן פֿאַלנדיקע ווענט
דאָס ליד געזונגען מיט נאַגאַנעס אין די הענט

Never say that you have reached your journey's end; that heavy clouds conceal the light of day. Upon us yet will dawn the day for which we yearn. Our tramping feet will then proclaim that we are here.

SHLOIMELE MALKELE

Music: J. Rumshinsky Lyrics: I. Lillian

Oy, Mal-ke-le ich bin m'-shu-ge far dir

©by J.J. Kammen Music

A shves-ter bin ich dir a tra-ye	א שוועסטער בין איך דיר א טרייע
Bru-derl her zich nor ain	ברודערל הער זיך נאר איין
A pik-tshe bis-tu a m'-cha-ye	א פיקטשע ביסטו א מחיה
Darf ich gor dain bru-der zain	דארף איך גאר דיין ברודער זיין
Bru-der 'ch-vel dich to-mid acht-en	ברודער כ׳וועל דיך תמיד אכטען
Az ich bin dain bru-der nit	אז איך בין דיין ברודער ניט
Oi shloi-me-le oi shloi-me-le	אוי שלמהלע אוי שלמהלע
Bru-der kum nen-ter tsu mir	ברודער קום נעהנטער צו מיר
Oy mal-ke-le oy mal-ke-le	אוי מלכהלע אוי מלכהלע
Ich bin m'-shu-ga far dir	איך בין משוגע פאר דיר

Oi! Shloimele, Oi! Malkele we really do not want a brother and sister relationship. The truth is that I am crazy about you and you about me!

ZOL SHOIN KUMEN DI G'ULA

Music A. I. Kook   Lyrics: S. Kaczerginski

Sh. Kaczerginski (1908-1954), Vilna poet, folklorist and partisan fighter, was among the first to collect and publish the songs of the ghettos and concentration camps. Written right after the holocaust and set to the music of Rabbi Abraham Isaac Kook (Chief Rabbi of Israel), *Zol Shoin Kumen Di G'ulo* expresses the eternal hope and longing for salvation.

On-ge-zol-yet oi-fn har-tsn macht men a l'-cha-yim
Oib der u-met lozt nit ru-en zing-en mir a lid
Iz ni-to kain bi-sl bron-fn, lo-mir trink-en ma-yim
Ma-yim cha-yim iz doch cha-yim—vos darf noch der Yid?

Refrain
Zol shoin ku-men di g'-u-lo
Mo-shi-ach kumt shoin bald!

'S-iz a dor fun ku-lo cha-yov zait nit kain na-ro-nim
Un fun zin-di-kn Mo-shi-ach gi-cher ku-men vet!
Ach du Ta-te-le in himl 's-bé-tn b'-né rach-mo-nim
Zé Mo-shi-ach zol nit ku-men a bi-se-le tsu shpét *Refrain:*

'S-tan-tsn bé-mer in di vel-der shtern oi-fn hi-ml
Reb Yis-ro-él der m'-chu-tn drét zich in der mit
'S-vet zich oif-ve-kn Mo-shi-ach fun zain ti-fn dri-ml
Ven er vet der-hern und-zer t'-fi-lo-di-ke lid *Refrain:*

אנגעזאליעט אויפן הארצן מאכט מען א לחיים
אויב דער אומעט לאזט ניט רוען זינגען מיר א ליד
איז ניטא קיין ביסל בראנפן-לאמיר טרינקען מַיִם
מַיִם חַיִּים איז דאך חַיִּים-וואס דארף נאך א ייד

רעפריין
זאל שוין קומען די גְּאוּלָה
מָשִׁיחַ קומט שוין באלד

ס'איז א דור פון כֻּלוֹ חַיָּב זייט ניט קיין נַעֲרָנִים
און פון זינדיקן-משיח גיכער קומען וועט
אך דו טאטעלע אין הימל ס'בעטן בני רַחֲמָנִים
זע משיח זאל ניט קומען א ביסעלע צו שפעט

ס'טאנצן ביימער איז די וועלדער שטערן אויפן הימל
ר' ישראל דער מחותן דרייט זיך אין דער מיט
ס'וועט זיך אויפוועקן משיח פון זיין טיפן דרימל
ווען ער וועט דערהערן אונדזער תפילהדיקע ליד

Though our hearts are ever aching, we will lift our cups to life. If there is no brandy then water will have to do. Salvation will soon come! The Messiah is on his way!

CHIRIBIM

Folk

oi chi-ri-bi-ri bi-ri bim bom bom   oi chi-ri bi-ri bi-ri bim bom bom

Az ich vel zing-en L'-cha do-di	אָז אִיךְ וֶועל זִינגען לְכָה דוֹדִי
Zolst du zing-en chiri-bi-ri-bim	זָאלסט דו זִינגען טשִׁירִי בִּירִי בִּים
Az ich vel zing-en lik-rat ka-la	אָז אִיךְ וֶועל זִינגען לִקְרַאת כַּלָה
Zolst du zing-en chiri-bi-ri-bom	זָאלסט דו זִינגען טשִׁירִי בִּירִי בָּם
L'-cha do-di chi-ri-bi-ri-bim	לְכָה דוֹדִי טשִׁירִי בִּירִי בִּים
Lik-rat ka-la chi-ri-bi-ri bom	לִקְרַאת כַּלָה טשִׁירִי בִּירִי בָּם
L'-cha do-di lik-rat ka-la	לְכָה דוֹדִי לִקְרַאת כַּלָה
Chiri-bi-ri-bi-ri-bi-ri bom	טשִׁירִי בִּירִי בִּירִי בִּירִי בָּם
U-ch'-she o-mar L'-cha do-di	וּכְשֶׁאָמַר לְכָה דוֹדִי
Tom-ru kul-chem chiri-bi-ri-bim	תֹּאמְרוּ כּוּלְכֶם טשִׁירִי בִּירִי בִּים
U-ch'-she o-mar lik-rat ka-la	וּכְשֶׁאָמַר לִקְרַאת כַּלָה
Tom-ru kul-chem chiri-bi-ri-bom	תֹּאמְרוּ כּוּלְכֶם טשִׁירִי בִּירִי בָּם
L'-cha do-di chiri-bi-ri-bim	לְכָה דוֹדִי טשִׁירִי בִּירִי בִּים
Lik-rat ka-la chiri-bi-ri-bom	לִקְרַאת כַּלָה טשִׁירִי בִּירִי בָּם
L'-cha do-di lik-rat ka-la	לְכָה דוֹדִי לִקְרַאת כַּלָה
Chiri-bi-ri-bi-ri-bi-ri bom	טשִׁירִי בִּירִי בִּירִי בִּירִי בָּם

When I say *L'cha Dodi* you will answer "Chiri-biri-bim." When I say *Likrat Kala* you will answer "Chiri-biri-bom."

DI M'ZINKE

Folktune

Originally titled *Di Rod*, the theme was used by Ernest Bloch in the Simchas Torah section of his *Baal Shem*. Very often at the wedding of the last daughter, the bride's parents sit, a garland is placed on the mother's head, and the guests dance *Di M'zinke Tantz* around them.

Allegro moderato

He-cher be-ser di rod di rod macht gre-ser

grois hot mich Got ge-macht glick hot er mir ge-bracht hul-yet kin-der a

gan-tse nacht di m'-zin-ke ois-ge-ge-ben di m'-zin-ke ois-ge-ge-ben

He-cher be-ser	העכער בעסער
Di rod di rod macht gre-ser	די ראד די ראד מאכט גרעסער
Grois hot mich got ge-macht	גרויס האט מיך גאט גמאכט
Glik hot er mir ge-bracht	גליק האט ער מיר געבראכט
Hul-yet kin-der a gan-tse nacht	הוליעט קינדער א גאנצע נאכט
Di m'-zin-ke ois-ge-gé-bn	די מיזינקע אויסגעגעבן
Shtar-ker fré-lech	שטארקער פריילעך
Du di mal-ka ich der mé-lech	דו די מַלְכָּה איך דער מֶלֶךְ
Oi oi ich a-lén	אוי אוי איך אליין
Hob mit mai-ne oi-gn ge-zén	האב מיט מיינע אויגן געזען
Vi Got hot mich mats-li-ach ge-vén	ווי גאט האט מיך מצליח געווען
Di m'-zin-ke ois-ge-gé-bn	די מיזינקע אויסגעגעבן

Louder, livelier! Make the circle wider. God has brought me good fortune. My youngest daughter is getting married. Dance and carry on throughout the night.

CHOSON KALA MAZEL TOV

This melody is often used as a wedding recessional.

Folktune

Cho-son ka-lo mazel tov
Vintsht a-le haint
A yom tov iz haint

חָתָן כַּלָה מזל טוב
ווינטשט אלע היינט
א יום טוב איז היינט

Bridegroom and bride mazel-tov! Today is a holiday!

YOSEL, YOSEL

Music: N. Casman Lyrics: S. Steinberg

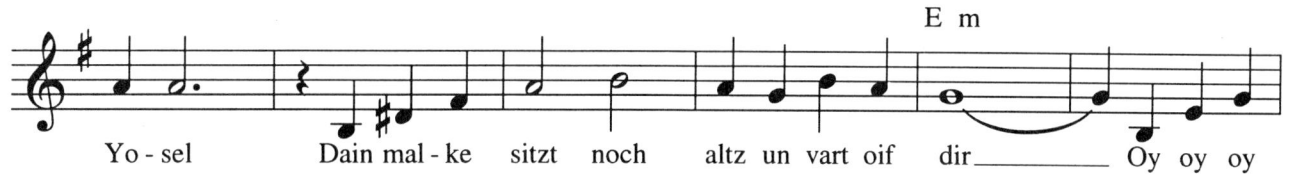
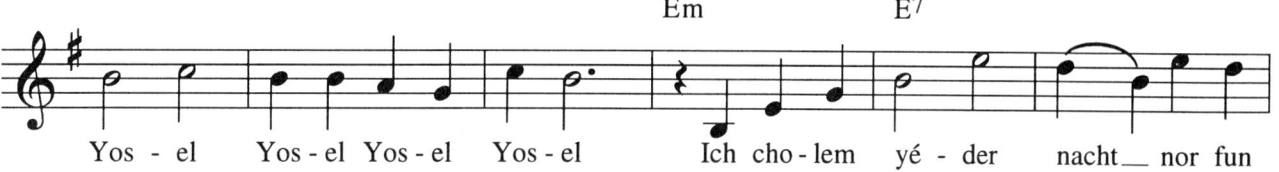

Main chai-es gét mir ois	מײן חיות געהט מיר אויס
Ich fil ich halt nit ois	איך פיהל איך האלט ניט אויס
Main harts tut mir vé	מײן הארץ טוט מיר וויי
Gor on a shir	גאר אהן א שיעור
Es iz mir hés un kalt	עס איז מיר הייס און קאלט
Un ich ver groi un alt	און איך ווער גרוי און אלט
Un vést ir ment-shn	און ווייסט איהר מענטשן
Vos es kvélt mir	וואס עס קווײלט מיר
Di li-be brent a shrek	די ליבעברענט א שרעק
Ich fil ich shtarb a-vek	איך פיהל איך שטארב אוועק
Noch main Yoslen	נאך מײן יוסלין מײן
Main "darling" main "dear"	"דארלינג" מײן "דיר"
A bo-chur a shé-ner	א בחור א שײנער
Mir zol zain far zai-ne béner	מיר זאל זײן פאר זײנע בײנער
Yosel ich kra-pir noch dir	יוסל איך קראפיר נאך דיר
Oy oy oy Yosel, Yosel, Yosel, Yosel	אוי אוי אוי יוסל, יוסל, יוסל
Main chai-es gét mir a-zhe ois far dir	מײן חיות געהט מיר אזע אויס פאר דיר
Oy oy oy Yosel, Yosel, Yosel, Yosel	אוי אוי אוי יוסל, יוסל, יוסל
Dain mal-ke zitst noch alts	דײן מַלכָּה זיצט נאך אלץ
Un vart far dir	און ווארט אויף דיר
Oy oy oy Yosel, Yosel, Yosel, Yosel	אוי אוי אוי יוסל, יוסל, יוסל
Ich cho-lem yé-der nacht nor fundir	איך חלום יעדער נאכט נאר פון דיר
In git der yé-tser ho-re	און גיט דער יצר הרע
Noch a mol a to-re	נאך א מאל א טארע
Yosel ich kra-pir noch dir	יוסל איך קראפיר נאך דיר

©by J.J. Kammen Music

RUMANIA RUMANIA

A. Lebedeff

One of the great favorites of the Yiddish stage was composed by Aaron Lebedeff over a period of years. He added and deleted material in response to his audiences. In a setting by Sholom Secunda, it was recorded by Lebedeff and a host of other Yiddish singers.

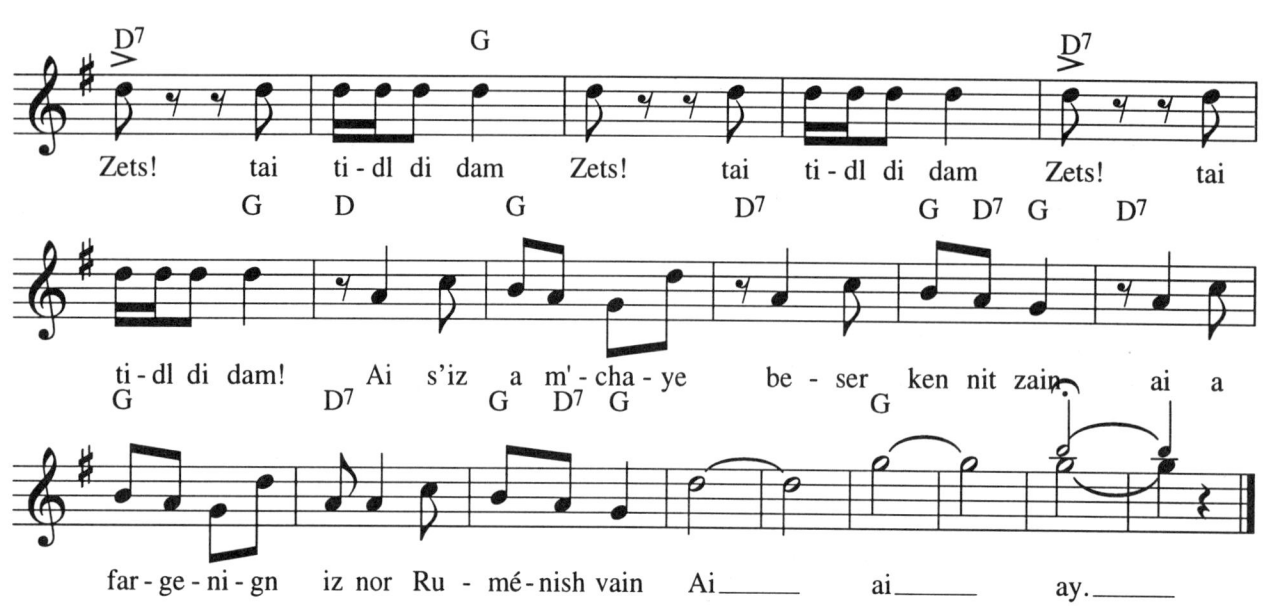

Ech Rumania Rumania........	עך רומעניע רומעניע............
Ge-ven a mol a land a zi-se a shé-ne	געווען א מאל א לאנד א זיסע א שיינע
Ech Rumania Rumania........	עך רומעניע רומעניע............
Ge-ven a mol a land a zi-se a fai-ne	געווען א מאל א לאנד א זיסע א פיינע
Dort tsu voi-nen iz a far-ge-ni-gen	דארט צו וואוינען איז א פארגעניגען
Vos dos hartz glust dir	וואס דאס הארץ גלוסט דיר
Dos ken-stu kri-gen	דאס קענסטו קריגען
A ma-me-li-ge-le a pas-tra-me-le	א מאמעליגעלע א פאסטראמעלע
A kar-na-tsa-le-le un a glé-ze-le vain	א קארנאצעלע און א גלעזעלע וויין
In Rumania iz doch git	אין רומעניע איז דאך גיט
Fun kain dai-ges vést men nit	פון קיין דאגעס ווייסט מען ניט
Vain trinkt men iber-al	וויין טרינקט מען איבעראל
Me far-baist mit kash-ta-val	מע פארבייסט מיט קאשטאוואל
Hai digidigigidigidam digidigigidigidam....	הי דיגידיגיאם דיגידיגידיגידאם.........
Oi ge-vald ich ver m'-shu-ga	אוי געוואלד איך ווער משוגע
'Ch lib nor brin-ze ma-me-li-ge	'כליב נאר ברינזע מאמעליגע
'Ch tantz un fré zich biz der stel-ye	'כטאנץ און פריי זיך ביז דער סטעליע
Ven ich es a pat-la-ze-le	ווען איך עס א פאטלאזעלע
Dzing ma tai ti-di-di dam....	דזינג-מא טיי טידידי דאם.........
Ai 's-iz a m'-cha-ye be-ser ken nit zain	אַי 'סאיז א מחיה בעסער קען ניט זיין
Ai a far-ge-ni-gen iz nor Ru-mé-nish vain	אי א פארגעניגען איז נאר רומעניש וויין
Y'-kum pur-kon min sh'-ma-yo	יְקוּם פּוּרְקָן מִן שְׁמַיָּא
Shtét un kusht di kech-ne cha-ye	שטייט און קושט די קעכנע חיה
On-ge-ton in al-te shkra-bes	אנגעטאן אין אלטע שקראבעס
Macht a ku-gel l'-ko-ved Sha-bos	מאכט א קוגעל לכבוד שבת
Tai tidldidam zets taitidldidam	טי טידלדידאם זעטס טידלדידאם.........
Ai 's iz a m'-cha-ye be-ser ken nit zain	אי 'סאיז א מחיה בעסער קען ניט זיין
Ai a far-ge-ni-gen iz nor Ru-mé-nish vain	אי א פארגעניגען איז נאר רומעניש וויין

Ah! Rumania Rumania. It was once a beautiful country. To live there was a pleasure. Pastrami, mamalige and above all wonderful wine.

SEPHARDIC

AND

ORIENTAL

CUANDO EL REY NIMROD

Ladino Folksong

Cuando el rey Nimrod al campo salia
Mirava en el cielo y en la estreyeria
Vido una luz santa en la giuderia
Que havia de nacer *Avraham avinu*
Avraham avinu padre querido
Padre bendicho luz de *Israel*

Saludemos al compadre y tambien al *moel*
Que por su *z'chut* mos venga el *goel*
Y ri'hma a todo *Israel*
Cierto loaremos al verdadero
Al verdadero de *Israel*

When King Nimrod went out into the fields
He looked at the heavens and at all the stars
He saw a holy light above the Jewish quarter
A sign that Abraham our father was about to be born
Abraham our father, beloved father
Blessed father, light of Israel

Let us greet the godfather and also the mohel
Because of his virtue may the Messiah come
To redeem all Israel
Surely we will praise the true redeemer
The true redeemer of Israel

LOS BILBILICOS

Ladino Folksong

This melody is known throughout the world wherever Sephardim reside. In many communities it has also been adpted to the liturgical *Zemira* text, *Tsur Mishelo Achalnu*, sung in the home at the first Sabbath meal on Friday night.

Los bilbilicos cantan
Con sospiros de amor
Mi neshama mi ventura
Estan en tu poder

La rosa enflorese
En el mes de mai
Mi neshama s'escurese
Sufriendo del amor

Mas presto ven palomba
Mas presto ven con mi
Mas presto ven querida
Corre y salvame

The nightingales sing
With sighs of love
My soul and my fate
Are in your power

The rose blooms
In the month of May
My soul and my fate
Suffer from love's pain

Come more quickly dove
More quickly come with me
More quickly come beloved
Run and save me

SCALERICA DE ORO

Ladino Folksong

Scalerica de oro, de oro y de marfil
Para que suva la novia a dar
Kidushin
Refrain
Venimos a ver, venimos a ver
Y gozen y logren y tengan
Muncho bien

La novia no tiene dinero
Que mos tenga un mazal bueno *Refrain*

La novia no tiene contado
Que mos tenga un mazal alto *Refrain*

A ladder of gold and ivory
So our little bride can go up to take
Her marriage vows.
Refrain
We've come to see, we've come to see
May they have joy and prosper
And always be happy

The bride has no money
May they have good fortune Refrain

The bride has no riches
May they have good luck Refrain

YO M'ENAMORI D'UN AIRE

Ladino Folksong

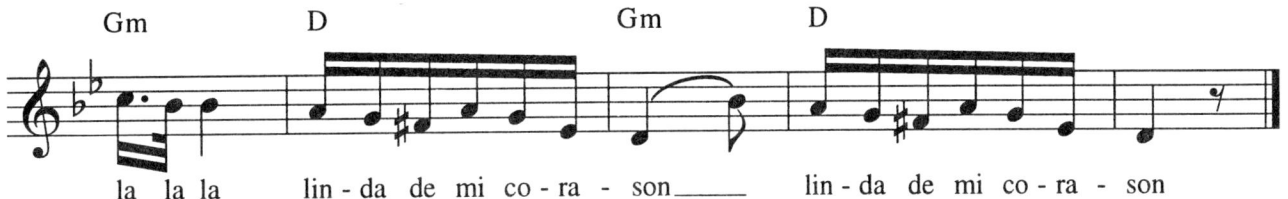

Yo m'enamori d'un aire ah-	I fell in love with the charms oh-
D'un aire d'una mujer	The charms of a woman
D'una mujer muy hermoza	Of a very beautiful woman
Linda de mi corason	The beauty of my heart
Yo m'enamori d'un aire ah-	I fell in love with the charms oh-
Linda de mi corason	The beauty of my heart
Tralala, lala.....	Tralala, lala..........
Linda de mi corason	The beauty of my heart
Yo m'enamori di noche ah-	I fell in love at night oh-
El lunar y m'engano	The moonlight was my undoing
Si esto era de dia	If it had been in daylight
Yo no atava amor	Love would not have bound me
Yo m'enamori de noche, ah-	I fell in love at night oh-
Yo no atava amor	Love would not have bound me
Tralala, lala.......	Tralala, lala........
Yo no atava amor	Love would not have bound me
Si otra vez m'enamoro ah-	If again I fall in love oh-
D'un aire d'una mujer	With the charms of a woman
D'una mujer muy hermoza	Of a very beautiful woman
Linda de mi corason	The beauty of my heart
Sea de dia con sol ah-	It will be by day with sunshine oh-
Si otra vez m'enamoro	If again I fell in love
Sea de dia con sol	It will be by day with sunshine oh-
Tralala., lala......	Tralala, lala...........
Si otra vez m'enamoro	If again I fell in love
Sea de dia con sol	It will be by day with sunshine

DURME, DURME

Traditional Ladino Folksong

Durme durme ijiko de madre
Durme durme sin ansia i dolor

Sienti djoia palavrikas de tu madre
Las palavras de Sh'ma Yisraél

Durme durme ijiko de madre
Kon ermozura de Sh'ma Yisraél

Sleep sleep mother's little boy
Free from worry and pain

Listen joy to your mother's words
The words of *Sh'ma Yisraél*

Sleep sleep mother's little boy
With the beauty of *Sh'ma Yisraél*

HITRAGUT

Oriental Folktune

Im yésh é sham ra-chok na-ve ka-tan sha-két
V'-lo g'-zuz-t'-ra shel éts v'-al ya-da sha-kéd
Im yésh é sham ra-chok v'-lu mé-ot par-sa
Sav-ta l'-nech-da-ta ta-shir ar-se-cha
Ki az a-uf l'-sham b'-a-chad ha-a-ra-vim
V'-shuv nim-ne yach-dav mis-par ha-ko-cha-vim

אִם יֵשׁ אֵי-שָׁם רָחוֹק נָוֶה קָטָן שָׁקֵט
וְלוֹ גְּזוּזְטְרָה שֶׁל עֵץ וְעַל יָדָהּ שָׁקֵד
אִם יֵשׁ אֵי-שָׁם רָחוֹק וְלוּ מֵאוֹת פַּרְסָה
סַבְתָּה לְנֶכְדָּתָהּ תָּשִׁיר עַרְשֶׂךָ
כִּי אָז אָעוּף לְשָׁם בְּאַחַד הָעֲרָבִים
וְשׁוּב נִמְנֶה יַחְדָּו מִסְפַּר הַכּוֹכָבִים

In the far distant land there is a quiet little dwelling with a wooden balcony and a grandmother singing a cradle song to her little one. I would fly there one evening and count the stars with her.

TA'AM HAMAN

Folktune   Lyrics: I. Navon

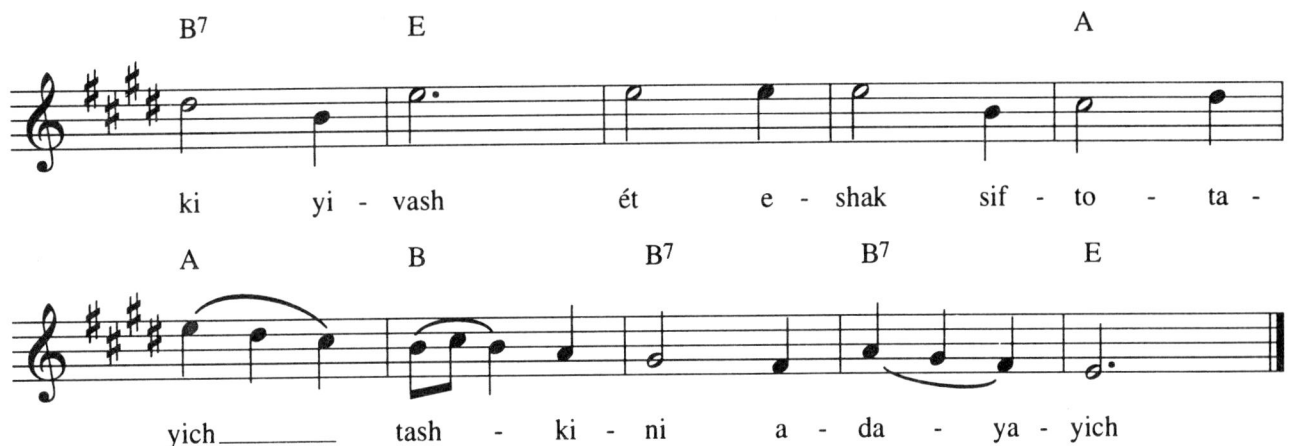

Giz-ra-téch tav-nit nu-ga
Ré-cha nérd uv-mor su-ga
Sif-to-ta-yich ar-ga-man
Ni-van bi-not ta-a-man man
Ta-am ha-man
Im y'-su-par lo y'-u-man
Tsuf ti-rosh cha-lav ud-vash
Lo yé-ra-vu-ni chi-ki yi-vash
Ét e-shak sif-to-ta-yich
Tash-ki-ni a-da-ya-yich

גִּזְרָתֵךְ תַּבְנִית נוֹגָה
רֵיחָהּ נֵרְדְּ וּבְמוֹר סוּגָה
שִׂפְתוֹתַיִךְ אַרְגָּמָן
נִיבָן בִּינוֹת טַעֲמָן מָן
טַעַם הַמָּן
אִם יְסֻפַּר לֹא יֵאָמֵן
צוּף תִּירוֹשׁ חָלָב וּדְבָשׁ
לֹא יְרַוּוּנִי חִכִּי יִיבָשׁ
עֵת אֶשַּׁק שִׂפְתוֹתַיִךְ
תַּשְׁקִינִי עֲדָיַיִךְ

Neither wine, nor milk, nor honey tempts me; only when I kiss your lips is my thirst quenched.

OCHO KANDELIKAS

F. Jagoda

In Yugoslavia on each of the eight nights of Hanuka "matchmaking parties" were held; and while the young people sang and danced, their parents and grandparents enjoyed planning their children's wedding. Little almond cakes were eaten to assure luck, happiness—and a good match!

©by the Author. All rights reserved

Hanuka linda sta aki
Ocho kandelas para mi   O
Refrain
Una kandelika, dos kandelikas
Tres kandelikas, kuatro kandelikas
Sintyu kandelikas, sej kandelikas
Siete kandelikas
Ocho kandelas para mi

Muchas fiestas vo fazer
Kon alegriyas i plazer   O....   *Refrain*
Los pastelikos vo kumer
Kon almendrikas i la myel   O... *Refrain*

Beautiful Hanuka is here
Eight candles for me O....
Refrain
One candle, two candles
Three candles, four candles
Five candles, six candles
Seven candles
Eight candles for me

Many parties I will have
With happiness and pleasure O... *Refrain*
The little pastries we will eat
Filled with almonds and honey O...*Refrain*

LANÉR V'LIVSAMIM

A. Medina

©by the Author. All rights reserved

La-nér v'-li-v'-sa-mim naf-shi m'-ya-ché-la
Im tit-nu li kos ya-yin l'-hav-da-la

לַנֵר וְלִבְשָׂמִים נַפְשִׁי מְיַחֵלָה
אִם תִּתְּנוּ לִי כּוֹס יַיִן לְהַבְדָלָה

My soul awaits the candle and the incense. If you should but give me a goblet of wine for Havdala.

MIZMOR L'DAVID

Sephardic Folktune   Lyrics: Liturgy

The two melodies for the *Mizmor L'david* text found in this edition are based on the same melodic motifs. Both are well known throughout the Sephardic communities. Many Ashkenazic synagogues have also incorporated these tunes into their Friday evening service.

Miz-mor l'-da-vid
Ha-vu la-do-nai b'-né é-lim
Ha-vu la-do-nai ka-vod va-oz
Ha-vu la-do-nai k'-vod sh'-mo
Hish-ta-cha-vu la-do-nai
B'-had-rat ko-desh
Kol A-do-nai al ha-ma-yim
Él ha-ka-vod hir-im
A-do-nai al ma-yim ra-bim
A-do-nai la-ma-bul ya-shav
Va-yé-shev A-do-nai me-lech l'-o-lam
A-do-nai oz l'-a-mo yi-tén
A-do-nai y'-va-réch et a-mo va-sha-lom

מִזְמוֹר לְדָוִד
הָבוּ לַיְיָ בְּנֵי אֵלִים
הָבוּ לַיְיָ כָּבוֹד וָעוֹז
הָבוּ לַיְיָ כְּבוֹד שְׁמוֹ
הִשְׁתַּחֲווּ לַיְיָ
בְּהַדְרַת קֹדֶשׁ
קוֹל יְיָ עַל הַמָּיִם
אֵל הַכָּבוֹד הִרְעִים
יְיָ עַל מַיִם רַבִּים
יְיָ לַמַּבּוּל יָשָׁב
וַיֵּשֶׁב יְיָ מֶלֶךְ לְעוֹלָם
יְיָ עֹז לְעַמּוֹ יִתֵּן
יְיָ יְבָרֵךְ אֶת עַמּוֹ בַשָּׁלוֹם

A psalm of David: Give to the Lord, O heavenly beings, give to the Lord honor and glory. Give to the Lord the glory due His name; worship the Lord in holy array. The voice of the Lord peals across the waters.

MIZMOR L'DAVID II

Sephardic Folktune   Lyrics: Liturgy

Miz-mor l'-da-vid	מִזְמוֹר לְדָוִד
Ha-vu la-do-nai b'-né é-lim	הָבוּ לַיְיָ בְּנֵי אֵלִים
Ha-vu la-do-nai ka-vod va-oz	הָבוּ לַיְיָ כָּבוֹד וָעוֹז
Ha-vu la-do-nai k'-vod sh'-mo	הָבוּ לַיְיָ כְּבוֹד שְׁמוֹ
Hish-ta-cha-vu la-do-nai	הִשְׁתַּחֲווּ לַיְיָ
B'-had-rat ko-desh	בְּהַדְרַת קֹדֶשׁ
Kol A-do-nai al ha-ma-yim	קוֹל יְיָ עַל הַמָּיִם
Él ha-ka-vod hir-im	אֵל הַכָּבוֹד הִרְעִים
A-do-nai al ma-yim ra-bim	יְיָ עַל מַיִם רַבִּים

A psalm of David: Give to the Lord, O heavenly beings, give to the Lord honor and glory. Give to the Lord the glory due His name; worship the Lord in holy array. The voice of the Lord peals across the waters.

YITSMACH SHALOM

I. Navon

Yits-mach sha-lom rav mé-ar-tsi
N'-vé sha-lom ir chem-da-ti
Chok u-mish-pat yiv-nu pir-tsi
Yo-du kol a-mim chén da-ti

יִצְמַח שָׁלוֹם רַב מֵאַרְצִי
נְוֵה שָׁלוֹם עִיר חֶמְדָּתִי
חֹק וּמִשְׁפָּט יִבְנוּ פִּרְצִי
יוֹדוּ כָּל עַמִּים חֵן דָּתִי

A great and lasting peace shall emanate from my homeland. All nations shall recognize the beauty of my religion.

ÉTS HARIMON

Adapted from a Persian melody by
Y. Gorchov and Y. Orland

From afar the soldier longs for his beloved land of Israel. Dark-eyed and of tinkling voice, she is more fair than all the girls he has known. Remembering her beauty he sings, "The arrow returns to its bow......"

©by the Authors. All rights reserved

Éts ha-ri-mon na-tan ré-cho
Bén yam ha-me-lach ad y'-ri-cho
Shav cho-ma-ti g'-du-déch min-dod
Shav ta-ma-ti do-déch mi-dod
Ots-rot o-fir uts-ri gil-ad
Re-chev mits-ra-yim sha-lal-ti lach bat
E-lef ha-ze-mer et-le lach ma-gén
Min ha-y'-or ad ha yar-dén

עֵץ הָרִמּוֹן נָתַן רֵיחוֹ
בֵּין יַם הַמֶּלַח עַד יְרִיחוֹ
שָׁב חוֹמָתִי גְדוּדֵךְ מִנְדוֹד
שָׁב תַּמָּתִי דּוֹדֵךְ מְדוֹד
אוֹצְרוֹת אוֹפִיר וְצֳרִי גִלְעָד
רֶכֶב מִצְרַיִם שָׁלַלְתִּי לָךְ בַּת
אֶלֶף הַזֶּמֶר אֶתְלֶה לָךְ מָגֵן
מִן הַיְאוֹר עַד הַיַּרְדֵּן

The arrow returns to its bow; the plucked pomegranate pines for the tree; so does this soldier yearn for his loved one. Wait for me dear, for evening descends.

YOM ZE L'YISRAÉL

Sephardic Folktune Lyrics: Z'mirot Liturgy

Yom ze l'-yis-ra-él
O-ra v'-sim-cha
Sha-bat m'-nu-cha

יוֹם זֶה לְיִשְׂרָאֵל
אוֹרָה וְשִׂמְחָה
שַׁבָּת מְנוּחָה

This day is for Israel -- a day of light and gladness, the Sabbath of rest.

KI ESHM'RA SHABAT

Oriental Folktune   Lyrics: Z'mirot Liturgy

This Sabbath *zmira*, table song, is also known throughout Oriental Jewish communities as *Ahavat Hadasa*. Its authorship is credited to Shalom Shabazi, one of the famous Yemenite poets.

Ki esh-m'-ra Sha-bat
El yish-m'-ré-ni
Ot hi l'-ol-mé ad
Bé-no u-vé-ni

כִּי אֶשְׁמְרָה שַׁבָּת
אֵל יִשְׁמְרֵנִי
אוֹת הִיא לְעוֹלְמֵי עַד
בֵּינוֹ וּבֵינִי

If I safeguard the Sabbath, God will safeguard me. It is a sign forever between Him and me.

YIGDAL

Spanish-Portuguese

Yigdal is recited in many synagogues both on Friday evening and during the daily morning service. The melody (also used for *Bendigamos*) is one of the best known in the Spanish-Portuguese Synagogue of Amsterdam, Holland and is used for a variety of texts with minor alterations and variations. (See *Az Yashir* Page 149)

Yig-dal E-lo-him chai v'-yish-ta-bach
Nim-tsa v'-én ét el m'-tsi-u-to
E-chad v'-én ya-chid k'-yi-chu-do
Ne-e-lam v'-én sof l'-ach-du-to

יִגְדַּל אֱלֹהִים חַי וְיִשְׁתַּבַּח
נִמְצָא וְאֵין עֵת אֶל מְצִיאוּתוֹ
אֶחָד וְאֵין יָחִיד כְּיִחוּדוֹ
נֶעְלָם וְאֵין סוֹף לְאַחְדוּתוֹ

Exalted and praised be the living God! He exists; His existence transcends time. He is the One-there is no oneness like his; He is unknowable-His oneness is endless.

D'ROR YIKRA

Oriental Folktune   Lyrics: Sabbath Z'mirot Liturgy

D'-ror yik-ra l'-vén im bat
V'-yin-tsar-chem k'-mo va-vat
N'-im shim-chem v'-lo yush-bat
Sh'-vu v'-nu-chu b'-yom Sha-bat

דְּרוֹר יִקְרָא לְבֵן עִם בַּת
וְיִנְצָרְכֶם כְּמוֹ בָבַת
נָעִים שִׁמְכֶם וְלֹא יִשְׁבַּת
שְׁבוּ וְנוּחוּ בְּיוֹם שַׁבָּת

He shall proclaim freedom for all and protect you. Rest and be contented on the Sabbath day.

143

D'ROR YIKRA II

Oriental Folktiune

D'-ror yik-ra l'-vén im bat
V'-yin-tsar-chem k'-mo va-vat
N'-im shim-chem v'-lo yush-bat
Sh'-vu v'-nu-chu b'-yom Sha-bat

דְּרוֹר יִקְרָא לְבֵן עִם בַּת
וְיִנְצָרְכֶם כְּמוֹ בָבַת
נְעִים שִׁמְכֶם וְלֹא יִשְׁבַּת
שְׁבוּ וְנוּחוּ בְּיוֹם שַׁבָּת

He shall proclaim freedom for all and protect you. Rest and be contented on the Sabbath day.

MA'OZ TSUR

Sephardic Folktune   Lyrics: Liturgy

This melody for *Ma'oz Tsur* was transcribed and preserved by B. Marcello, an Italian composer who documented a number of melodies of the Italian Sephardim.

Ma-oz tsur y'-shu-a-ti
L'-cha na-e l'-sha-bé-ach
Ti-kon bét t'-fi-la-ti
V'-sham to-da n'-za-bé-ach
L'-ét ta-chin mat-bé-ach
Mi-tsar ham-na-bé-ach
Az eg-mor
B'-shir miz-mor
Cha-nu-kat ha-miz-bé-ach

מָעוֹז צוּר יְשׁוּעָתִי
לְךָ נָאֶה לְשַׁבֵּחַ
תִּכּוֹן בֵּית תְּפִלָּתִי
וְשָׁם תּוֹדָה נְזַבֵּחַ
לְעֵת תָּכִין מַטְבֵּחַ
מִצָּר הַמְנַבֵּחַ
אָז אֶגְמוֹר
בְּשִׁיר מִזְמוֹר
חֲנֻכַּת הַמִּזְבֵּחַ

O God, my saving stronghold, to praise You is a delight. Restore my house of prayer where I will offer You thanks. When You will prepare havoc for the foe who maligns us, I will gratify myself with a song at the altar.

KADÉSH UR'CHATS

Oriental Folktune

Ka-désh ur-chats, kar-pas ya-chats
Ma-gid rach-tsa, mo-tsi ma-tsa
Ma-ror ko-réch, shul-chan o-réch
Tsa-fun ba-réch, ha-lél nir-tsa

קַדֵּשׁ וּרְחַץ כַּרְפַּס יַחַץ
מַגִּיד רָחְצָה מוֹצִיא מַצָּה
מָרוֹר כּוֹרֵךְ שֻׁלְחָן עוֹרֵךְ
צָפוּן בָּרֵךְ הַלֵּל נִרְצָה

The order of the Passover Seder.

KADÉSH URCHATS II

Oriental Folktune

Ka-désh ur-chats, kar-pas ya-chats
Ma-gid rach-tsa, mo-tsi ma-tsa
Ma-ror ko-réch, shul-chan o-réch
Tsa-fun ba-réch, ha-lél nir-tsa

קַדֵּשׁ וּרְחַץ כַּרְפַּס יַחַץ
מַגִּיד רָחְצָה מוֹצִיא מַצָּה
מָרוֹר כּוֹרֵךְ שֻׁלְחָן עוֹרֵךְ
צָפוּן בָּרֵךְ הַלֵּל נִרְצָה

The order of the Passover Seder.

QUEN SUPIESE Y

A charming version of *Echad Mi Yode'a*, Who Knows One, sung in Judeo-Espagnol, the Ladino language.

Ladino Folktune

Quen supiese y entendiense, alavar al Dio creense cualo es el uno: Uno es el Criador, Baruch hu, baruch sh'mo
Quen supiese y entendiense alavar al Dio creense cualos son los dos:
Dos Moshe y Aron, Uno es el Criador, Baruch hu baruch sh'mo
Cualos son los tres: tres padres muestros son: Avram Yitzchak, Yaakov, Dos Moshe ....
Cualos son los cuatro: Cuatro madres muestras son: Sara, Rivka, Leah, Rachel, Tres muestros padres. ....
Cualos son los cinco- cinco livros de la Ley etc
Cualos son los seij- seij dias de la semana, cinco etc..
Cualos son los siete- siete dias con Shabat, seij, etc.
Cualos son los ocho- ocho dias de la mila, siete, etc..
Cualos son los mueve- mueve mezes de la prenada, etc.
Cualos son los diez- diez mandamientos de la Ley, etc..
Cualos son los onze- onze trivos sin Yosef, diez, etc .....
Cualos son los doze- doze trivos con Yosef, onze, etc ....

Who knows One? I know one. One is our God who is in heaven and on earth.
Who knows two?..... two are the tablets.....three are the forefathers,
four are the mothers, five are the Books of Moses etc.

AZ YASHIR MOSHE

Spanish & Portuguese Foltune   Lyrics: Liturgy

From the Spanish-Portuguese synagogue in Holland comes this melody for the *Shira,* the Song of the Red Sea. *Az Yashir* is chanted on the Sabbath and holidays. The song is said to be quite old but nothing is known about the composer or date of origin.

Az ya-shir Mo-she u-v'-né Yis-ra-él
Et ha-shi-ra ha-zot la-do-nai
Va-yo-m'-ru lé-mor
A-shi-ra la-do-nai ki ga-o ga-a
Sus v'-roch-vo ra-ma va-yam

אָז יָשִׁיר מֹשֶׁה וּבְנֵי יִשְׂרָאֵל
אֶת הַשִּׁירָה הַזֹּאת לַיְיָ
וַיֹּאמְרוּ לֵאמֹר
אָשִׁירָה לַיְיָ כִּי גָאֹה גָּאָה
סוּס וְרֹכְבוֹ רָמָה בַיָּם

Then Moses and the children of Israel sang this song to the Lord; they said: I will sing to the Lord for He has triumphed; the horse and its rider He has hurled into the sea.

NON KOMO MUESTRO DYO

A version of the liturgical text En Kelohnu interspersed with Ladino phrases widely known in Yugoslavia and a special favorite of young people.

Traditional   Lyrics: Liturgy

Én ke-lo-hé-nu én ka-do-né-nu
Én k'-mal-ké-nu én k'-mo-shi-é-nu
Non ko-mo mues-tro Dyo,
Non komo muestro Sinyor
Non ko-mo mues-tro Ré
Non ko-mo mues-tro Sal-va-dor

There is none like our God
There is none like our Lord
There is none like our King
There is none like our Deliverer

AMÉN SHEM NORA

Spanish-Portuguese Folktune   Lyrics: Festival Liturgy

A festive hymn sung on the eve of Simchat Torah following the regular service, as part of the *Hakafot* (circuits). *Amen Shem Nora* is also popular in Holland as one of the traditional table songs for the Shabbat. In recent years it has become popularized among both Western and Oriental Sephardim.

A-mén shem no-ra
El a-dir no-ra v'-a-yom
L'-am-cha t'-na fid-yon
Vi-va-réch et-chem ha-yom
V'-a-mar kol ha-am a-mén

אָמֵן שֵׁם נוֹרָא
אֵל אַדִּיר נוֹרָה וְאָיוֹם
לְעַמְּךָ תְּנָה פִדְיוֹן
וִיבָרֵךְ אֶתְכֶם הַיּוֹם
וְאָמַר כָּל הָעָם אָמֵן

May the almighty God bless his people this day and let us all say amen.

MI PI ÉL

Oriental Folktune

Mi Pi El is widely sung in the Oriental Jewish community. The text, which extols the virtues of God, Moses, the Torah and the Jewish people, is also sung by Ashkenazic Jews especially on the night of Simchat Torah during the processional of the scrolls.

En a-dir ka-do-nai
V'-én ba-ruch k'-ven a-m'-ram
En g'-vi-ra ka-to-ra
En do-r'-she-ha k'-yis-ra-él
Mi pi Él mi pi Él
Y'-vo-rach Yis-ra-él

אֵין אַדִיר כַּיְיָ
וְאֵין בָּרוּךְ כְּבֶן עַמְרָם
אֵין גְּבִירָה כַּתּוֹרָה
אֵין דּוֹרְשָׁהּ כְּיִשְׂרָאֵל
מִפִּי אֵל מִפִּי אֵל
יְבֹרַךְ יִשְׂרָאֵל

There is no one greater than God. There is no one more blessed than Moses. There is nothing greater than the Tora. There are no people as wonderful as the people of Israel.

HAMAVDIL

The Havdala service closes the Sabbath celebration. The ceremony conducted with candles, wine and incense closes the Sabbath and introduces the new work week.

Oriental Folktune

Ha-mav-dil bén ko-desh l'-chol	הַמַּבְדִּיל בֵּין קֹדֶשׁ לְחוֹל
Cha-to-té-nu yim-chol	חַטֹּאתֵינוּ יִמְחוֹל
Zar-é-nu v'-chas-pé-nu	זַרְעֵנוּ וְכַסְפֵּנוּ
Yar-be ka-chol	יַרְבֶּה כַחוֹל
Ka ko-cha-vim ba-lai-la	כַּכּוֹכָבִים בַּלַּיְלָה
Lich-vod chem-dat l'-va-vi	לִכְבוֹד חֶמְדַּת לְבָבִי
E-li-ya-hu ha-na-vi	אֵלִיָּהוּ הַנָּבִיא

May He who separates the holy from the secular forgive our sins; may He increase our offspring and our wealth as the stars.

IN

ENGLISH

MOMELE

M. Parish, A. Alstone & A. Goodhart

As I watch you light the Sabbath candles
There's a lovely glow upon your face
While you're standing there whispering a prayer
None can take your place
Momele, momele
Mother dear I'll always call you momele
Tired eyes, wrinkled hands
And the loving heart that always understands
I remember how you used to comfort me
A little girl of three in bygone years
I remember how you took me on your knee
With a kiss you dry all my tears
Silver hair, heart of gold
Day by day I hate to see you growing old
Momele, Momele
May God bless you mome mine

LEAVING MOTHER RUSSIA

R. Solomon

Performed by the group Safam, *Leaving Mother Russia* became an anthem during the long struggle by Jews to leave Russia. It was a favorite among Jewish college students throughout the United States and by organizations dedicated to the release of Jews from the Soviet Union.

- sia___ when they come for us___ we'll be gone

©by the Author. All rights reserved

They called me Anatole in prison I did lie
My little window looked out on a Russian sky
For nearly nine long years secluded and in pain
I've been arrested here for crimes they have not named
And all my people know the charges were a frame
I see my accuser standing in the hall
He points his finger at us all
You now must pay the penalty
For the crime of daring to be free.

   Refrain
   We are leaving Mother Russia
   We have waited far too long
   We are leaving Mother Russia
   When they come for us we'll be gone

Through all the centuries we called this land our home
We loved the Russian soil as much as anyone
In countless armies our young boys have died for you
But never did you call them "sons"
You always called them "Jew"!
We fell in battle for the Tsar
One hundred thousand died at Babi Yar
And yet you monument will denies their faith
While on our passports we read "Yevrai"   *Refrain*

I send my song of hope to those I left behind
I pray that they may know the freedom that is mine
For through my darkest hours alone inside my cell
I kept the vision of my home in Yisrael
My friends we know what silence brings
Another Hitler waiting in the wings
So stand up now and shout it to the sky—
Though they bring us to our knees
We will never die!   *Refrain*

JERUSALEM IS MINE

K. Karen

I am the sun Jerusalem, you are a painted sky
I am a bird Jerusalem, you have the wings to fly
You are the father of my dream, I am the gift of time
I am your child Jerusalem, Jerusalem is mine

You are the orchard in the sand, I am the fruit you bear
You are the glove that warms my hands, I am the smile you wear
You are the music of the hills, I am the words that rhyme
I am your song Jerusalem, Jerusalem is mine

You are the cradle of freedom, I am the harvest of Springtime
You are the dawn of a new day, I am tomorrow, you are forever
You are my shelter from the storm, I am your guiding light
You are a book whose leaves are torn, I am the page you write
You are the branches of a tree, I am a clinging vine
I am a prayer Jerusalem, Jerusalem is mine
I have come home Jerusalem, Jerusalem is mine.

DONA DONA

Music: Sholom Secunda   Lyrics: Sheldon Secunda

Originally entitled *"Dana, dana, dana,"* the song was published in 1943. It became one of the most widely sung Yiddish songs and was peformed In Yiddish and English translation by Theodore Bikel, Joan Baez and others. Translations have also appeared in German and Korean.

© by the authors. All rights reserved

On a wagon bound for market
There's a calf with a mournful eye
High above him there's a swallow
Winging swiftly through the sky
Refrain
How the winds are laughing
They laugh with all their might
Laugh and laugh the whole day through
And half a summer's night
Donna donna donna ....

"Stop complaining," said the farmer
"Who told you a calf to be
Why don't you have wings to fly with
Like the swallow so proud and free?" *Refrain*

Calves are easily bound and slaughtered
Never knowing the reason why
But whoever treasures freedom
Like the swallow has learned to fly   *Refrain*

Oi-fen furl ligt dos kel-bel
Ligt ge-bun-den mit a shtrik
Hoich in him-el flit dos shvel-bel
Frét zich drét zich hin un krik
Refrain
Lacht der vint in korn
Lacht un lacht un lacht
Lacht er op a tog a gan-tsen
Mit a hal-ber nacht
Dona dona dona........

Shrait dos kel-bel zogt der poi-er
Ver zhe hést dich zain a kalb
Volst ge-kert tsu zain a foi-gel
Volst ge-kert tsu zain a shvalb *Refrain*

Kel-ber tut men bin-den
Un men shlept zé un men shecht
Ver s'hot fli-gel flit a-roif-tsu
Iz bai ké-nem nit kain knecht *Refrain*

אויפן פורל ליגט דאס קעלבל
ליגט געבונדן מיט א שטריק
הויך אין הימל פליט דאס שוועלבל
פרייט זיך דרייט זיך הין און קריק
רעפריין
לאכט דער ווינט אין קארן
לאכט און לאכט און לאכט
לאכט ער אפ א טאג א גאנצן
מיט א האלבער נאכט
דאנא, דאנא, דאנא.........

שרייט דאס קעלבל זאגט דער פויער
ווער זשע הייסט דיך זיין א קאלב?
וואלסט געקערט צו זיין א פויגל
וואלסט געקערט צו זיין א שוואלב רעפריין

קעלבער טוט מען בינדן
און מען שלעפט זיי און מען שעכט
ווער ס׳האט פליגל פליט ארויפצו
איז ביי קיינעם ניט קיין קנעכט רעפריין

163

L'CHI LACH

Debbie Friedman

Debbie Friedman is one of the the best known artists in contemporary Jewish music. Her recordings and music books have received world-wide acclaim.

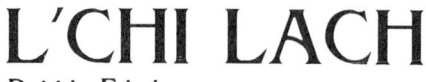

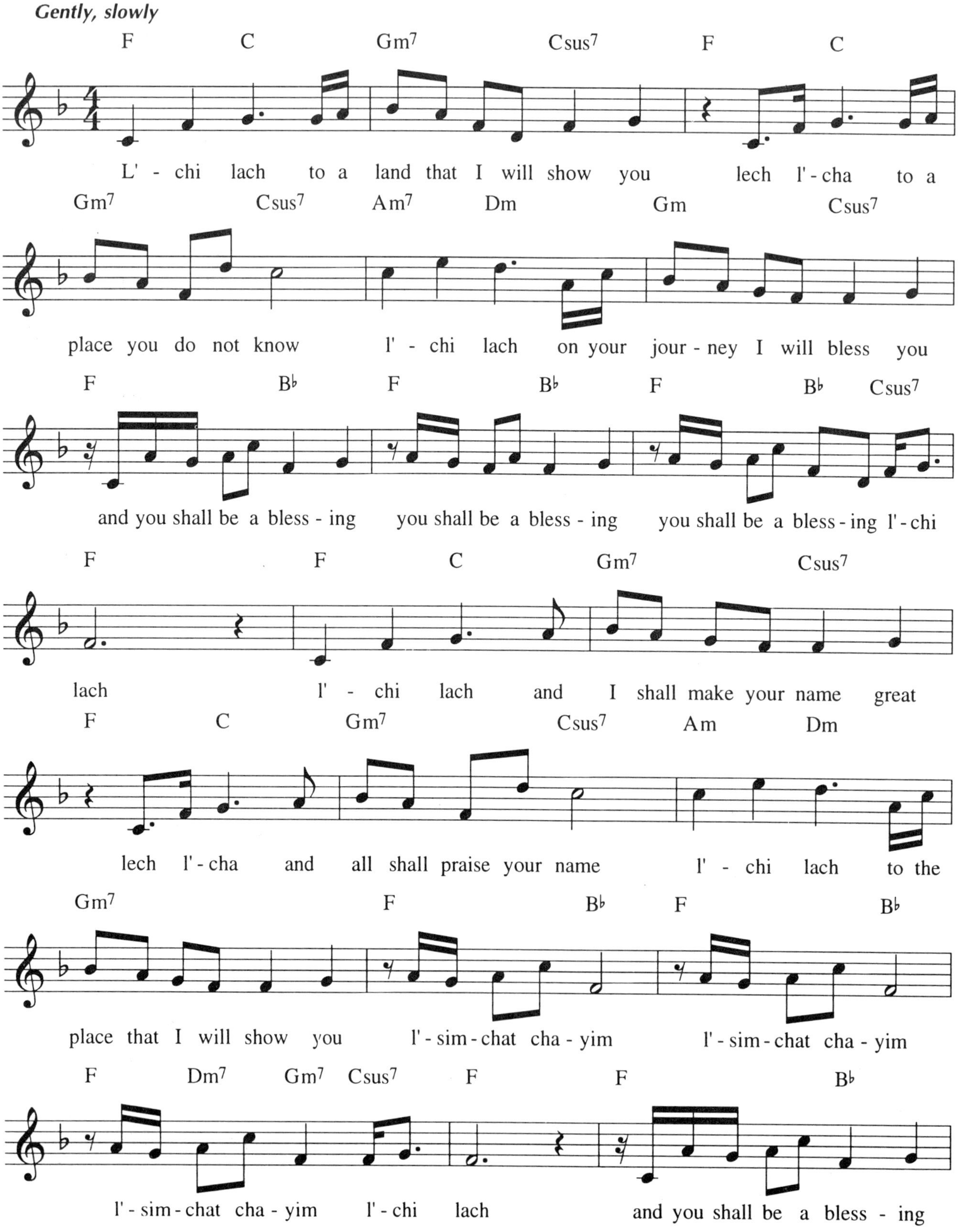

Gently, slowly
F C Gm7 Csus7 F C
L' - chi lach to a land that I will show you lech l'-cha to a
Gm7 Csus7 Am7 Dm Gm Csus7
place you do not know l' - chi lach on your jour - ney I will bless you
F B♭ F B♭ F B♭ Csus7
and you shall be a bless - ing you shall be a bless - ing you shall be a bless-ing l'-chi
F F C Gm7 Csus7
lach l' - chi lach and I shall make your name great
F C Gm7 Csus7 Am Dm
lech l'-cha and all shall praise your name l' - chi lach to the
Gm7 F B♭ F B♭
place that I will show you l'-sim-chat cha-yim l'-sim-chat cha-yim
F Dm7 Gm7 Csus7 F F B♭
l'-sim-chat cha-yim l'-chi lach and you shall be a bless - ing

©by the Author. All rights reserved

L'chi lach, to a land that I will show you
Lech l'cha, to a place you do not know
L'chi lach, on your journey I will bless you
And you shall be a blessing, *l'chi lach*

L'chi lach, and I shall make your name great
Lech l'cha, and all shall praise your name
L'chi lach, to the place that I will show you
L*'simchat chayim l'chi lach*

LIGHT ONE CANDLE

P. Yarrow

Composed by Peter Yarrow of "Peter, Paul and Mary" fame, this is one of the group's most often performed songs. It has become a favorite world-wide.

Light one candle for the Maccabee children
Give thanks that their light didn't die
Light one candle for the pain they endured
When their right to exist was denied
Light one candle for the terrible sacrifice
Justice and freedom demand
Light one candle for the wisdom to know
When the peace-maker's time is at hand
> *Refrain*
> Don't let the light go out
> It's lasted for so many years
> Don't let the light go out
> Let it shine through our love and our tears
> Don't let the light go out

Light one candle for the strength that we need
To never become our own foe
Light one candle for those who are suffering
The pain we learned so long ago
Light one candle for the all we believe in
Let anger not tear us apart
Light one candle to bind us together
With peace as the song in our heart   *Refrain*

What is the memory that's valued so highly
That we keep alive in that flame
What's the commitment to those who have died
When we cry out "they've not died in vain."
We have come this far always believing
That justice will somehow prevail
This is the burden and this is the promise
And this is why we will not fail   *Refrain*

MY ZÉDI

Megama

©by the Author. All rights reserved

My zédi lived with us in my parents home
He used to laugh, he put me on his knee
And he spoke about his life in Poland
He spoke with a bitter memory
And he spoke about the soldiers who would beat him
They laughed at him, they tore his long black coat
And he spoke about a synagogue that they burned down
And the crying that was heard beneath the smoke
But zédi made us laugh, zédi made us sing
And Zedi made the kidush Friday night
And zédi O my zédi how I loved him so
And zédi used to teach me wrong from right.

His eyes lit up when he would teach me Torah
He taught me every line so carefully
He spoke about our slavery in Egypt
And how God took us out to make us free
But winter went by, summer came along
I went to camp to run and play
And when I came back home they said zédi's gone
And all his books were packed and stored away.

I don't know how or why it came to be
It happened slowly over many years
We just stopped being Jewish like my zédi was
And no one cared enough to shed a tear
But zédi made us laugh, zédi made us sing
And zédi made a Seder Pesach night
And zédi O my zédi how I loved him so
And zédi used to teach me wrong from right.

Many winters went by, many summers came along
And now my children sit in front of me
And who will be the zédi of my children
Who will be their zédi if not me
Who will be the zédis of our children
Who will be their zédis if not we
And zédi made us laugh, zédi made us sing
And Zedi made the kidush Friday night
And zédi O my zédi how I loved him so
And zédi used to teach me wrong from right.

ALEF BET
Debbie Friedman

* **Echo effect**

©by the Author. All rights reserved

Let's learn the *Alef bet* simple as it can be
You'll learn the *Alef bet* if you sing the letters after me
Each letter has a name and a sound it always makes
Now let's sing this special chorus we'll have fun it will not bore us
It's the *Alef bet*
Alef bet vet gimel dalet hé vav zayin chet tet yud kaf chaf
Lamed mem nun samech ayin pé fé tsadi kuf résh shin sin taf

SABBATH

AND

HOLIDAYS

SHABAT HAMALKA

Music: P. Minkowsky   Lyrics. C. N. Bialik

© by the authors. All rights reserved

Ha-cha-ma mé-rosh ha-i-la-not nis-tal-ka
Bo-u v'-né-tsé lik-rat Sha-bat ha-mal-ka
Hi-né hi yo-re-det hak'-do-sha ha-b'-ru-cha
V'-i-ma mal-a-chim ts'-va sha-lom u-m'-nu-cha
Bo-i bo-i ha-mal-ka bo-i bo-i ha-ka-la
Sha-lom a-lé-chem mal-a-ché ha-sha-lom

הַחַמָּה מֵרֹאשׁ הָאִילָנוֹת נִסְתַּלְּקָה
בֹּאוּ וְנֵצֵא לִקְרַאת שַׁבָּת הַמַּלְכָּה
הִנֵּה הִיא יוֹרֶדֶת הַקְּדוֹשָׁה הַבְּרוּכָה
וְעִמָּהּ מַלְאָכִים צְבָא שָׁלוֹם וּמְנוּחָה
בֹּאִי בֹּאִי הַמַּלְכָּה בֹּאִי בֹּאִי הַכַּלָּה
שָׁלוֹם עֲלֵיכֶם מַלְאֲכֵי הַשָּׁלוֹם

The sun on the tree tops no longer is seen. Come gather to welcome the Sabbath our queen. Behold her descending, the holy the blest and with her the angels of peace and rest. Draw near O Sabbath bride. Peace be with you angels of peace.

Y'DID NEFESH

Music S. & E. Zweig Lyrics: Liturgy

One of the song winners at an early Israeli Chassidic Song Festival, *Y'did Nefesh* has become a permanent part of the Jewish song repertoire. It is often used as a processional at traditional weddings.

Y'-did ne-fesh av ha-ra-cha-man © by the authors. All rights reserved
M'-shoch av-d'-cha el r'-tso-ne-cha
Ya-ruts av-d'-cha k'mo a-yal
Yish-ta-cha-ve el mul ha-da-re-cha
Ye-e-rav lo y'-di-do-te-cha
Mi-no-fet tsuf v'-chol ta-am

ידיד נֶפֶשׁ אָב הָרַחֲמָן
מְשׁוֹךְ עַבְדְּךָ אֶל רְצוֹנֶךָ
יָרוּץ עַבְדְּךָ כְּמוֹ אַיָּל
יִשְׁתַּחֲוֶה אֶל מוּל הֲדָרֶךָ
יֶעֱרַב לוֹ יְדִידוֹתֶיךָ
מְנוֹפֶת צוּף וְכָל טַעַם

Beloved of the soul, merciful Father, draw Your servant unto Your will,
that swift as a hart may he run to prostrate himself before your majesty.

L'CHA DODI

Folktune

The origins of this tune are unknown. It is thought to be an Israeli kibbutz melody which spread to far-flung Jewish communities where it has become standard for this Friday evening liturgical text.

Refrain
L'-cha do-di lik-rat ka-la
P'-né Sha-bat n'-ka-b'-la

Sha-mor v'-za-chor b'-di-bur e-chad
Hish-mi-a-nu Él ha-m'-yu-chad
A-do-nai e-chad u-sh'-mo e-chad
L'-shém ul-tif-e-ret v'-lit-hi-la

פזמון
לְכָה דוֹדִי לִקְרַת כַּלָּה
פְּנֵי שַׁבָּת נְקַבְּלָה

שָׁמוֹר וְזָכוֹר בְּדִבּוּר אֶחָד
הִשְׁמִיעָנוּ אֵל הַמְיֻחָד
יְיָ אֶחָד וּשְׁמוֹ אֶחָד
לְשֵׁם וּלְתִפְאֶרֶת וְלִתְהִלָּה

Come my friend to meet the bride; let us welcome the Sabbath. "Observe" and "Remember" in a single command, the One God announced to us. The Lord is One, and His name is One, for fame, glory and for praise.

L'CHA DODI II

Music: M. Zeira Lyrics: Liturgy

©Mifalei Tarbuth Vechinuch

L'-cha do-di lik-rat ka-la
P'-né Sha-bat n'-kab-la
Sha-bat sha-lom u-m'-vo-rach

לְכָה דוֹדִי לִקְרַאת כַּלָּה
פְּנֵי שַׁבָּת נְקַבְּלָה
שַׁבָּת שָׁלוֹם וּמְבוֹרָךְ

Come let us welcome in joy the Sabbath bride.
A peaceful and a blessed Sabbath.

ADON OLAM

Music: U. Hitman   Lyrics: Liturgy

Uzi Hitman entered this melody in an Israel Chassidic Song Festival competition. It has became popular throughout the Jewish community world-wide.

A-don o-lam a-sher ma-lach
B'-te-rem kol y'-tsir niv-ra
L'-ét na-a-sa b'-chef-tso kol
A-zai me-lech sh'-mo nik-ra
V'-a-cha-ré kich-lot ha-kol
L'-va-do yim-loch no-ra
V'-hu ha-ya v'-hu ho-ve
V'-hu yi-ye b'-tif-a-ra

אֲדוֹן עוֹלָם אֲשֶׁר מָלַךְ
בְּטֶרֶם כָּל יְצִיר נִבְרָא
לְעֵת נַעֲשָׂה בְחֶפְצוֹ כֹּל
אֲזַי מֶלֶךְ שְׁמוֹ נִקְרָא
וְאַחֲרֵי כִּכְלוֹת הַכֹּל
לְבַדּוֹ יִמְלוֹךְ נוֹרָא
וְהוּא הָיָה וְהוּא הֹוֶה
וְהוּא יִהְיֶה בְּתִפְאָרָה

He is the eternal Lord who reigned before any being was created. At the time when all was made by His will, He was at once acknowledged as King. And at the end, when all shall cease to be, the revered God alone shall still be King. He was, He is and He shall be in glorious eternity.

ADON OLAM II

Traditional

A-don o-lam a-sher ma-lach
B'-te-rem kol y'-tsir niv-ra
L'-ét na-a-sa b'-chef-tso kol
A-zai me-lech sh'-mo nik-ra

אֲדוֹן עוֹלָם אֲשֶׁר מָלַךְ
בְּטֶרֶם כָּל יְצִיר נִבְרָא
לְעֵת נַעֲשָׂה בְּחֶפְצוֹ כֹּל
אֲזַי מֶלֶךְ שְׁמוֹ נִקְרָא

He is the eternal Lord who reigned before any being was created. At the time when all was made by His will, He was at once acknowledged as King.

SHABAT SHALOM

S. Secunda

Although commonly thought of as a folk melody, *Shabbat Shalom* is a song by Shalom Secunda, well-known theatrical conductor and composer of the 20th century.

©by the Author. All rights reserved

Sha-bat sha-lom

שַׁבָּת שָׁלוֹם

A peaceful Sabbath.

SHALOM ALÉCHEM

Music: S. E. Goldfarb Lyrics: Liturgy

Shalom Alechem is often thought to be a folk song of unknown authorship. Samuel Goldfarb's melody is known throughout the world and is often used for other texts in the Sabbath liturgy. (In many synagogues it is sung to *V'enenu Tirena* in the *K'dusha* of the *Shacharit* service.)

©by the Author. All rights reserved

Sha-lom a-lé-chem mal-a-ché ha-sha-rét mal-a-ché el-yon
Mi-me-lech mal-ché ham-la-chim ha-ka-dosh baruch hu
Bo-a-chem l'-sha-lom mal-a-ché ha-shalom mal-a-ché el-yon
Mi-me-lech mal-ché ham-la-chim ha-ka-dosh ba-ruch hu
Bar-chu-ni l'-shal-om mal-a-ché ha-shalom mal-a-ché el-yon
Mi-me-lech mal-ché ham-la-chim ha-ka-dosh ba-ruch hu
Tsét-chem l'-sha-lom mal-a-ché ha-shalom mal-a-ché el-yon
Mi-me-lech mal-ché ham-la-chim ha-ka-dosh ba-ruch hu

שָׁלוֹם עֲלֵיכֶם מַלְאֲכֵי הַשָּׁרֵת מַלְאֲכֵי עֶלְיוֹן
מִמֶּלֶךְ מַלְכֵי הַמְּלָכִים הַקָּדוֹשׁ בָּרוּךְ הוּא
בּוֹאֲכֶם לְשָׁלוֹם מַלְאֲכֵי הַשָּׁלוֹם מַלְאֲכֵי עֶלְיוֹן
מִמֶּלֶךְ מַלְכֵי הַמְּלָכִים הַקָּדוֹשׁ בָּרוּךְ הוּא
בָּרְכוּנִי לְשָׁלוֹם מַלְאֲכֵי הַשָּׁלוֹם מַלְאֲכֵי עֶלְיוֹן
מִמֶּלֶךְ מַלְכֵי הַמְּלָכִים הַקָּדוֹשׁ בָּרוּךְ הוּא
צֵאתְכֶם לְשָׁלוֹם מַלְאֲכֵי הַשָּׁלוֹם מַלְאֲכֵי עֶלְיוֹן
מִמֶּלֶךְ מַלְכֵי הַמְּלָכִים הַקָּדוֹשׁ בָּרוּךְ הוּא

Peace be upon you, angels of the Exalted One, from the King, the Holy One blessed be He. May your coming be for the sake of peace. Bless me for peace; and may your departure as well be with peace.

ÉSHET CHAYIL

B. Z. Shenker Lyrics: Liturgy

This poem, the traditional tribute to the Jewish woman, is recited before the Kidush on Friday evening. The melody by Ben Zion Shenker is known world-wide and is often thought of as a folk tune.

181

É-shet cha-yil mi yim-tsa
V'-ra-chok mip-ni-nim mich-ra
Ba-tach ba lév ba-la
V'-sha-lal lo yech-sar
G'-ma-lat-hu tov v'-lo ra
Kol y'-mé cha-ye-ha
Dar-sha tse-mer u-fish-tim
Va-ta-as b'-ché-fets ka-pe-ha
Hai-ta ka-a-ni-ot so-chér
Mi-mer-chak ta-vi lach-ma
Va-ta-kam b'-od lai-la
Va-ti-tén te-ref l'-vé-ta
V'-chok l'-na'-ro-te-ha
Za-m'-ma sa-de va-ti-ka-ché-hu
Mi-pri cha-pe-ha nat'-a ka-rem
Chag-ra b'-oz mat-ne-ha
Va-t'-a-méts z'-ro-o-te-ha

אֵשֶׁת חַיִל מִי יִמְצָא
וְרָחוֹק מִפְּנִינִים מִכְרָהּ
בָּטַח בָּהּ לֵב בַּעְלָהּ
וְשָׁלָל לֹא יֶחְסָר
גְּמָלַתְהוּ טוֹב וְלֹא רָע
כָּל יְמֵי חַיֶּיהָ
דָּרְשָׁה צֶמֶר וּפִשְׁתִּים
וַתַּעַשׂ בְּחֵפֶץ כַּפֶּיהָ
הָיְתָה כָּאֳנִיּוֹת סוֹחֵר
מִמֶּרְחָק תָּבִיא לַחְמָהּ
וַתָּקָם בְּעוֹד לַיְלָה
וַתִּתֵּן טֶרֶף לְבֵיתָהּ
וְחֹק לְנַעֲרֹתֶיהָ
זָמְמָה שָׂדֶה וַתִּקָּחֵהוּ
מִפְּרִי כַפֶּיהָ נָטְעָה כָּרֶם
חָגְרָה בְעוֹז מָתְנֶיהָ
וַתְּאַמֵּץ זְרוֹעֹתֶיהָ

A good wife who can find? She is worth far more than rubies. Her husband trusts in her and he never lacks gain.

YA RIBON

Folktune   Lyrics: Z'mirot Liturgy

Ya ri-bon a-lam v'-al-ma-ya
Ant hu mal-ka me-lech mal-cha-ya
O-vad g'-vur-téch v'-tim-ha-ya
Sh'-far ko-da-mach l'-ha-cha-va-ya

יָהּ רִבּוֹן עָלַם וְעָלְמַיָּא
אַנְתְּ הוּא מַלְכָּא מֶלֶךְ מַלְכַיָּא
עוֹבַד גְּבוּרְתֵּךְ וְתִמְהַיָּא
שְׁפַר קֳדָמָךְ לְהַחֲוַיָּא

Master of the world and of all worlds, You are the King who reigns over all kings. It is wonderful to declare your powerful deeds.

TSUR MISHELO

Music: Folk   Lyrics: Z'mirot liturgy

Tsur mi-she-lo a-chal-nu
Ba-r'-chu e-mu-nai
Sa-va-nu v'-ho-tar-nu
Kid-var A-do-nai

צוּר מִשֶּׁלּוֹ אָכַלְנוּ
בָּרְכוּ אֱמוּנַי
שָׂבַעְנוּ וְהוֹתַרְנוּ
כִּדְבַר יְיָ

Let us bless the Lord whose food we ate. Let us thank Him with our lips, chanting; There is no one holy like our Lord.

SHIR HAMA'ALOT

Before Hatikvah was selected as the national anthem of Israel, serious consideration was given to this melody composed by the famous cantor "Yossele" Rosenblatt.

Music: J. Rosenblatt Lyrics: Psalm 126

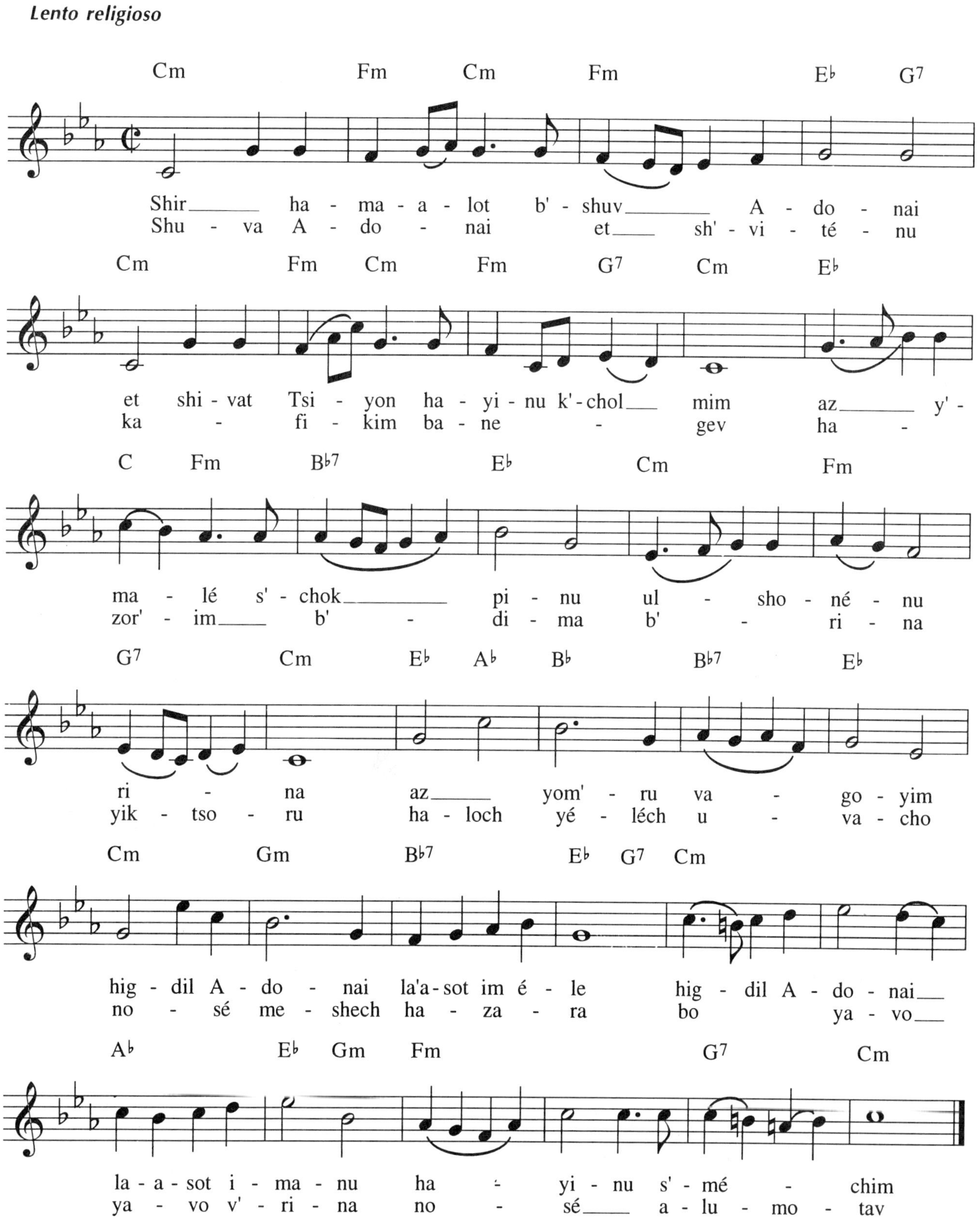
Lento religioso
Cm Fm Cm Fm E♭ G7
Shir ha - ma - a - lot b' - shuv A - do - nai
Shu - va A - do - nai et sh' - vi - té - nu
Cm Fm Cm Fm G7 Cm E♭
et shi - vat Tsi - yon ha - yi - nu k' - chol mim az y' -
ka - fi - kim ba - ne - gev ha -
C Fm B♭7 E♭ Cm Fm
ma - lé s' - chok pi - nu ul - sho - né - nu
zor' - im b' - di - ma b' - ri - na
G7 Cm E♭ A♭ B♭ B♭7 E♭
ri - na az yom' - ru va - go - yim
yik - tso - ru ha - loch yé - léch u - va - cho
Cm Gm B♭7 E♭ G7 Cm
hig - dil A - do - nai la'a - sot im é - le hig - dil A - do - nai
no - sé me - shech ha - za - ra bo ya - vo
A♭ E♭ Gm Fm G7 Cm
la - a - sot i - ma - nu ha - yi - nu s' - mé - chim
ya - vo v' - ri - na no - sé a - lu - mo - tav

Shir ha-ma-a-lot b'-shuv A-do-nai
Et shivat Tsi-yon ha-yi-nu k'-chol-mim
Az yi-ma-lé s'-chok pi-nu ul-sho-né-nu ri-na
Az yom'-ru va-go-yim
Hig-dil A-do-nai la'-sot im é-le
Hig-dil A-do-nai la-a-sot i-ma-nu
Ha-yi-nu s'-mé-chim
Shu-va A-do-nai et sh'-vi-té-nu
Ka-a-fi-kim ba-ne-gev
Ha-zor'-im b'-di-ma b'-ri-na yik-tso-ru
Ha-loch yé-lech u-va-cho
No-sé me-shech ha-za-ra
Bo ya-vo ya-vo v'-ri-na
No-sé a-lu-mo-tav

שִׁיר הַמַּעֲלוֹת בְּשׁוּב יְיָ
אֶת שִׁיבַת צִיּוֹן הָיִינוּ כְּחוֹלְמִים
אָז יִמָּלֵא שְׂחוֹק פִּינוּ וּלְשׁוֹנֵנוּ רִנָּה
אָז יֹאמְרוּ בַגּוֹיִם
הִגְדִּיל יְיָ לַעֲשׂוֹת עִם אֵלֶּה
הִגְדִּיל יְיָ לַעֲשׂוֹת עִמָּנוּ
הָיִינוּ שְׂמֵחִים
שׁוּבָה יְיָ אֶת שְׁבִיתֵנוּ
כַּאֲפִיקִים בַּנֶּגֶב
הַזֹּרְעִים בְּדִמְעָה בְּרִנָּה יִקְצֹרוּ
הָלוֹךְ יֵלֵךְ וּבָכֹה
נֹשֵׂא מֶשֶׁךְ הַזָּרַע
בֹּא יָבֹא בְרִנָּה
נֹשֵׂא אֲלֻמֹּתָיו

SHIR HAMA'ALOT II

Folktune   Lyrics: Psalm 126

ÉLIYAHU HANAVI

Folktune

In many Jewish communities it has been customary to sing about Elijah the Prophet at the time of the Havdala ceremony. Elijah represents the symbolic hope for the Messianic Age, a period of peace and justice, a universal Sabbath for mankind.

E-li-ya-hu ha-navi
E-li-ya-hu ha-tish-bi
E-li-ya-hu ha-gil-a-di
Bim-hé-ra v'ya-mé-nu
Ya-vo é-lé-nu
Im Ma-shi-ach ben David

אֵלִיָּהוּ הַנָּבִיא
אֵלִיָּהוּ הַתִּשְׁבִּי
אֵלִיָּהוּ הַגִּלְעָדִי
בִּמְהֵרָה בְיָמֵנוּ
יָבֹא אֵלֵינוּ
עִם מָשִׁיחַ בֶּן דָּוִד

Elijah the prophet, Elijah the Tishbite, Elijah the Gilead, may he soon come to us with the Messiah son of David.

SISU V'SIMCHU

Music: Y. Paikov   Lyrics: Liturgy

Si-su v'sim-chu b'-sim-chat Tora
Ut'-nu ka-vod la-to-ra

שִׂישׂוּ וְשִׂמְחוּ בְּשִׂמְחַת תּוֹרָה
וּתְנוּ כָּבוֹד לַתּוֹרָה

Let us rejoice altogether on Simchat Tora and give honor to God's Tora.

CANDLE BLESSINGS (HANUKA)

Traditional

Before the candles are lit on the first night of Hanuka, the Festival of Lights, all three blessings are recited. On all remaining nights, only verses 1 and 2 are said.

Ba-ruch a-ta A-do-nai E-lo-hé-nu me-lech ha-o-lam:
1. A-sher kid-sha-nu b'mits-vo-tav v'tsi-va-nu
L'-had-lik nér shel Cha-nu-ka.
2. She-a-sa ni-sim la-a-vo-té-nu
Ba-ya-mim ha-hém baz-man ha-ze.
3. She-he-che-ya-nu v'-ki-ma-nu
V'-hi-gi-a-nu laz-man ha-ze.

בָּרוּךְ אַתָּה יְיָ אֱלֹהֵינוּ מֶלֶךְ הָעוֹלָם:
1. אֲשֶׁר קִדְּשָׁנוּ בְּמִצְוֹתָיו וְצִוָּנוּ
לְהַדְלִיק נֵר שֶׁל חֲנֻכָּה.
2. שֶׁעָשָׂה נִסִּים לַאֲבוֹתֵינוּ
בַּיָּמִים הָהֵם בַּזְּמַן הַזֶּה.
3. שֶׁהֶחֱיָנוּ וְקִיְּמָנוּ
וְהִגִּיעָנוּ לַזְּמַן הַזֶּה.

Blessed are You, Lord our God, King of the universe, who has commanded us to kindle the Chanukah light; who wrought miracles for our fathers in those days; who gave us life and brought us to this season.

MA'OZ TSUR II

Traditional

Much has been written about the origins of this melody. Musicologists agree that it is an adopted non-Jewish tune. It is one of the best examples of a foreign melody becoming one of the best known and accepted tunes in Jewish life.

Ma-oz Tsur y'-shu-a-ti
L'-cha na-e l'-sha-bé-ach
Ti-kon bét t'-fi-la-ti
V'-sham to-da n'-za-bé-ach
L'-ét ta-chin mat-bé-ach
Mi-tsar ham-na-bé-ach
Az eg-mor
B'-shir miz-mor
Cha-nu-kat ha-miz-bé-ach

מָעוֹז צוּר יְשׁוּעָתִי
לְךָ נָאֶה לְשַׁבֵּחַ
תִּכּוֹן בֵּית תְּפִלָּתִי
וְשָׁם תּוֹדָה נְזַבֵּחַ
לְעֵת תָּכִין מַטְבֵּחַ
מִצָּר הַמְנַבֵּחַ
אָז אֶגְמוֹר
בְּשִׁיר מִזְמוֹר
חֲנֻכַּת הַמִּזְבֵּחַ

O God, my saving stronghold, to praise you is a delight. Restore my house of prayer where I will offer you thanks. When you will prepare havoc for the foe who maligns us, I will gratify myself with a song at the altar.

MI Y'MALÉL

Folktune adapted by M. Ravina
English lyrics: E. M. Edidin

Round

Mi y'-ma-lél g'vu-rot Yis-ra-él o-tan mi yim-ne hén b'-chol dor ya-kum ha-gi-bor go-él ha-am sh'ma ba-ya-mim ha-hém baz-man ha-ze ma-ka-bi mo-shi-a u-fo-de uv-ya-mé-nu kol am Yis-ra-él yit-a-chéd ya-kum v'-yi-ga-él

Mi y'-ma-lél g'-vu-rot Yisraél o-tan mi yim-ne
Hén b'-chol dor ya-kum ha-gi-bor go-él ha-am
Sh'-ma ba-ya-mim ha-hém baz-man ha-ze
Ma-ka-bi mo-shi-a u-fo-de
Uv-ya-mé-nu kol am Yisraél
Yit-a-chéd ya-kum v'-yi-ga-él

מִי יְמַלֵּל גְּבוּרוֹת יִשְׂרָאֵל אוֹתָן מִי יִמְנֶה
הֵן בְּכָל דּוֹר יָקוּם הַגִּבּוֹר גּוֹאֵל הָעָם
שְׁמַע בַּיָּמִים הָהֵם בַּזְּמַן הַזֶּה
מַכַּבִּי מוֹשִׁיעַ וּפוֹדֶה
וּבְיָמֵינוּ כָּל עַם יִשְׂרָאֵל
יִתְאַחֵד יָקוּם וְיִגָּאֵל

Who can retell the things that befell us
Who can count them?
In ev'ry age, a hero or sage
Arose to our aid.
Hark! In days of yore
In Israel's ancient land
Brave Macabeus led the faithful band
But now all Israel must as one arise
Redeem itself through deed and sacrifice.

S'VIVON

Folktune

In Israel the last line is sung with the words *nés gadol haya po* - a great miracle happened <u>here</u>.

S'vi-von sov sov sov Cha-nu-ka hu chag tov
Cha-nu-ka hu chag tov s'vi-von sov sov sov
Chag sim-cha hu la-am nés ga-dol ha-ya sham
Nés ga-dol ha-ya sham chag sim-cha hu la-am

סְבִיבוֹן סֹב סֹב סֹב חֲנֻכָּה הוּא חַג טוֹב
חֲנֻכָּה הוּא חַג טוֹב סְבִיבוֹן סֹב סֹב סֹב
חַג שִׂמְחָה הוּא לָעָם נֵס גָּדוֹל הָיָה שָׁם
נֵס גָּדוֹל הָיָה שָׁם חַג שִׂמְחָה הוּא לָעָם

Little dreydl, spin, spin, spin. Chance is a day of joy. Great was the miracle that happened there. Spin little dreydl spin, spin, spin.

Y'MÉ HACHANUKA

Folktune

The song is also known as *Chanuka Oy Chanuka a Yom Tov A Shener*. The Hebrew version presented here is a translation of the original Yiddish.

Y'-mé ha-cha-nu-ka cha-nu-kat mik-da-shé-nu
B'-gil u-v'-sim-cha m'-mal-im et li-bé-nu
Lai-la va-yom s'vi-vo-né-nu yi-sov
Suf-ga-ni-yot no-chal bam la-rov
Ha-i-ru had-li-ku né-rot Cha-nu-ka ra-bim
Al ha-ni-sim v'-al ha-nif-la-ot
A-sher cho-l'-lu ha-ma-ka-bim

יְמֵי הַחֲנֻכָּה חֲנֻכַּת מִקְדָּשֵׁנוּ
בְּגִיל וּבְשִׂמְחָה מְמַלְאִים אֶת לִבֵּנוּ
לַיְלָה וָיוֹם סְבִיבוֹנֵנוּ יִסֹּב
סֻפְגָּנִיּוֹת נֹאכַל בָּם לָרֹב
הָאִירוּ הַדְלִיקוּ נֵרוֹת חֲנֻכָּה רַבִּים
עַל הַנִּסִים וְעַל הַנִּפְלָאוֹת
אֲשֶׁר חוֹלְלוּ הַמַּכַּבִּים

O Chanuka, O Chanuka, come light the menora
Let's have a party we'll all dance the hora
Gather round the table we'll give you a treat
Shiny tops to play with and pancakes to eat
And while we are playing the candles are burning low
One for each night they shed a sweet light
To remind us of days long ago.

HINÉ BA

Music: G.F. Handel

A melody by George Frederick Handel from his oratorio *Judas Macabeus*.

Hi-né ba b'-hod tok-fo
Ba-cha-tsot-rot ho-du lo
Shi-ru zamru kol p'-du-yav
Shi-rat ni-tsa-chon é-lav

הִנֵּה בָּא בְּהוֹד תָּקְפּוֹ
בַּחֲצוֹצְרוֹת הוֹדוּ לוֹ
שִׁירוּ זַמְּרוּ כָּל פְּדוּיָו
שִׁירַת נִצָּחוֹן אֵלָיו

See the conquering hero comes
Sound the trumpets beat the drums
Sports prepare the laurels bring
Songs of triumph to him sing.

CHANUKA

Folktune

Cha-nu-ka chag ya-fe kol kach
Or cha-viv mi-sa-viv
Gil l'-ye-led rach
Cha-nu-ka s'vi-von sov sov
Ma na-im va-tov

חֲנֻכָּה חַג יָפֶה כָּל כָּךְ
אוֹר חָבִיב מִסָּבִיב
גִּיל לְיֶלֶד רַךְ
חֲנֻכָּה סְבִיבוֹן סֹב סֹב
מַה נָּעִים וְטוֹב

Chanuka is a merry holiday. Tops spin 'round, candles burn. O, let us sing and dance.

I HAVE A LITTLE DREYDL

Folksong

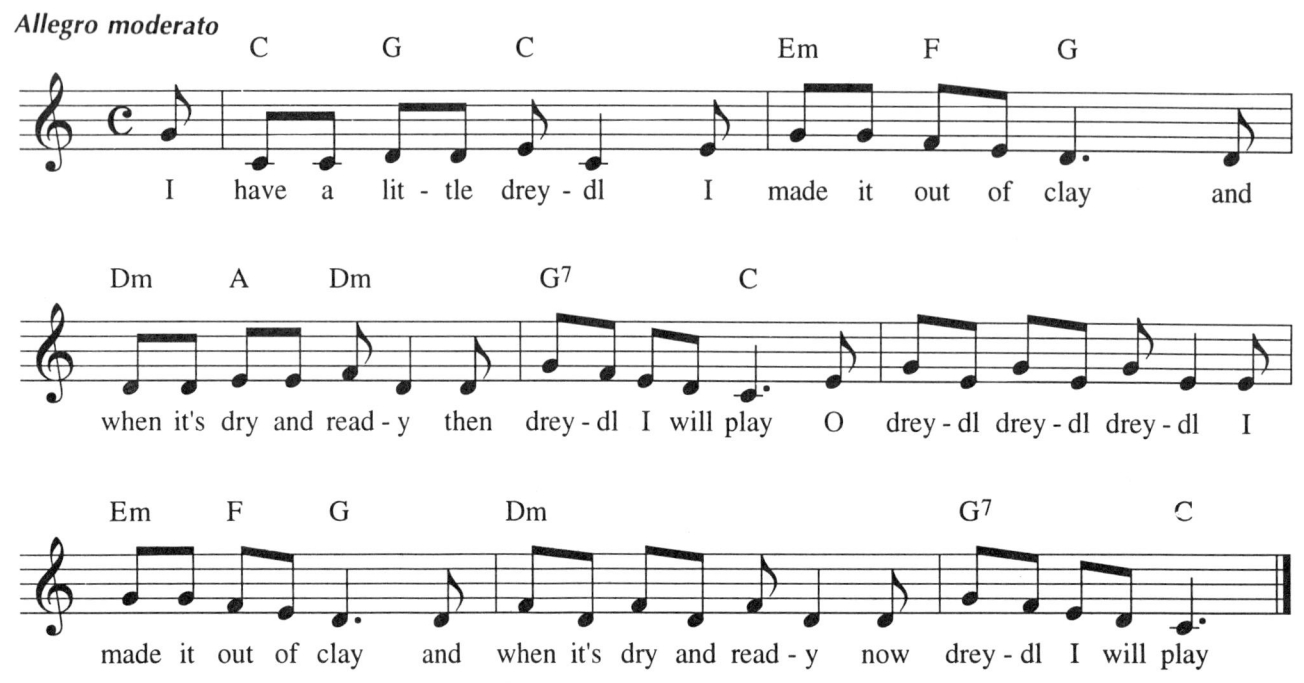

I have a little dreydl
I made it out of clay
And when it's dry and ready
Then dreydl I will play
O dreydl dreydl dreydl
I made it out of clay
And when it's dry and ready
Now dreydl I will play

It has a lovely body
With leg so short and thin
And when it is all tired
It drops and then I win
O dreydl dreydl dreydl
With leg so short and thin
And when it gets all tired
It drops and then I win.

My dreydl's always playful
It loves to dance and spin
A happy game of dreydl
Come play now let's begin
O dreydl dreydl dreydl
It loves to dance and spin
A happy game of dreydl
Come play now let's begin

TU BISHVAT

Folktune

Hash-ké-di-ya po-ra-chat
V'-she-mesh paz zo-ra-chat
Tsi-po-rim mé-rosh kol gag
M'-vas-rot et bo he-chag
Tu bish-vat hi-gi-a
Chag ha-i-la-not

הַשְׁקֵדִיָה פּוֹרַחַת
וְשֶׁמֶשׁ פָּז זוֹרַחַת
צִפָּרִים מֵרֹאשׁ כָּל גַג
מְבַשְׂרוֹת אֶת בֹּא הֶחָג
טוּ בִּשְׁבָט הִגִּיעַ
חַג הָאִילָנוֹת

The almond tree is growing and a golden sun is glowing. From every rooftop the birds sing out. Tu Bishvat is here, the New Year of the trees.

ANI PURIM

Folktune

A-ni Purim sa-mé-ach um-va-dé-ach
Ha-lo rak pa-am ba-sha-na a-vo l'-hit-a-ré-ach   la la...

Hé-dad Purim ha-ku tof um-tsil-ta-yim
Hoi mi yi-tén u-va Purim l'-cho-desh l'-chod-sha-yim   la la ...

Ra-bi Purim e-mor na li ma-du-a
Ma-du-a lo ya-chul Pu-rim pa-a-ma-yim ba-sha-vu-a   la la....

אֲנִי פּוּרִים שָׂמֵחַ וּמְבַדֵּחַ
הֲלֹא רַק פַּעַם בַּשָּׁנָה אָבוֹא לְהִתְאָרֵחַ ל ל ל......

הֵידָד פּוּרִים הַכּוּ תוֹף וּמְצִלְתַּיִם
הוֹי מִי יִתֵּן וּבָא פּוּרִים לְחֹדֶשׁ לְחָדְשַׁיִם ל ל ל......

רַבִּי פּוּרִים אֱמֹר נָא לִי מַדּוּעַ
מַדּוּעַ לֹא יָחוּל פּוּרִים פַּעֲמַיִם בַּשָּׁבוּעַ

How sad that Purim festivities come but once a year. Wouldn't it be fun if Purim came every month or, better yet, twice a week!

CHAG PURIM

Folktune

Chag Pu-rim chag ga-dol hu la-y'hu-dim
Ma-sé-chot ra-a-sha-nim z'mi-rot ri-ku-dim
Ha-va na-ri-sha rash rash rash
Ba-ra-a-sha-nim

חַג פּוּרִים חַג גָּדוֹל הוּא לַיְהוּדִים
מַסֵכוֹת רַעֲשָׁנִים זְמִירוֹת רִיקוּדִים
הָבָה נַרְעִישָׁה רַשׁ רַשׁ רַשׁ
בָּרַעֲשָׁנִים

The holiday of Purim is a great day for Jews. There are masks, groggers, songs and dances. Come let's make noise with our groggers.

HA LACHMA ANYA

Music: Y. Admon Lyrics: Seder Liturgy

Ha lach-ma an-ya di a-cha-lu av-ha-ta-na
B'-ar-a d'-mits-ra-yim
Kol dits-rich yé-té v'-yé-chul
Kol dich-fin yé-té v'-yif-sach
Ha-sha-ta ha-cha
L'-sha-na ha-ba-a b'-ar-a d'-yis-ra-él
Ha-sha-ta av-dé
L'-sha-na ha-ba-a b'-né cho-rin

©by the Author.

הָא לַחְמָא עַנְיָא דִּי אֲכָלוּ אַבְהָתָנָא
בְּאַרְעָא דְמִצְרָיִם
כָּל דִּכְפִין יֵיתֵי וְיֵיכֹל
כָּל דִּכְפִין יֵיתֵי וְיִפְסַח
הָשַׁתָּא הָכָא
לְשָׁנָה הַבָּאָה בְּאַרְעָא דְיִשְׂרָאֵל
הָשַׁתָּא עַבְדֵי
לְשָׁנָה הַבָּאָה בְּנֵי חוֹרִין

This is the bread of affliction which our forefathers ate in the land of Egypt. All who are hungry—come and eat. All who are hungry—come and celebrate Passover with us.

MA NISHTANA

Traditional

This is the traditional recitative version in the "question and answer" style of Talmud study.

Freely, in recitative style

Ma nish-ta-na ha-lai-la ha-ze__ mi-kol ha-lé-lot__ sheb'-chol ha-lé-lot a-nu och-

lin cha-méts u-ma-tsa__ ha-lai-la ha-ze__ ku-lo ma-tsa__

Repeat in similar fashion for additional verses

Ma nish-ta-na ha-lai-la ha-ze	מַה נִּשְׁתַּנָּה הַלַּיְלָה הַזֶּה
Mi-kol ha-lé-lot	מִכָּל הַלֵּילוֹת
She-b'chol ha-lé-lot a-nu och-lin	שֶׁבְּכָל הַלֵּילוֹת אָנוּ אוֹכְלִין
Cha-méts u-ma-tsa	חָמֵץ וּמַצָּה
Ha-lai-la ha-ze ku-lo ma-tsa	הַלַּיְלָה הַזֶּה כֻּלּוֹ מַצָּה
She-b'chol ha-lé-lot a-nu och-lin	שֶׁבְּכָל הַלֵּילוֹת
Sh'ar y'ra-kot	אָנוּ אוֹכְלִין שְׁאָר יְרָקוֹת
Ha-lai-la ha-ze ku-lo ma-ror	הַלַּיְלָה הַזֶּה כֻּלּוֹ מָרוֹר
She-b'-chol ha-lé-lot	שֶׁבְּכָל הַלֵּילוֹת
En a-nu mat-bi-lin a-fi-lu pa-am a-chat	אֵין אָנוּ מַטְבִּילִין אֲפִילוּ פַּעַם אֶחָת
Ha-lai-la ha-ze sh'-té f'-a-mim	הַלַּיְלָה הַזֶּה שְׁתֵּי פְעָמִים
She-b'-chol ha-lé-lot a-nu och-lin	שֶׁבְּכָל הַלֵּילוֹת
Bén yosh-vin	אָנוּ אוֹכְלִין בֵּין יוֹשְׁבִין
U-vén m'-su-bin	וּבֵין מְסֻבִּין
Ha-lai-la ha-ze ku-la-nu m'-su-bin	הַלַּיְלָה הַזֶּה כֻּלָּנוּ מְסֻבִּין

Why is this night different from all other nights? On this night why do we eat matza and bitter herbs; dip parsley in salt water and horseradish in charoset; and why do we recline at the table when we eat?

MA NISHTANA II

Folktune

In contrast to the recitative style of the other *Ma Nishtana* presented in this edition (page 201) this is a popular version of unknown origin. It is the favored melody at present because it is more melodic, rhythmical and singable by groups.

Ma nish-ta-na ha-lai-la ha-ze
Mi-kol ha-lé-lot
She-b'chol ha-lé-lot a-nu och-lin
Cha-méts u-ma-tsa
Ha-lai-la ha-ze ku-lo ma-tsa

מַה נִּשְׁתַּנָה הַלַּיְלָה הַזֶּה
מִכָּל הַלֵּילוֹת
שֶׁבְּכָל הַלֵּילוֹת אָנוּ אוֹכְלִין
חָמֵץ וּמַצָּה
הַלַּיְלָה הַזֶּה כֻּלּוֹ מַצָּה

Why is this night different from all other nights? On this night why do we eat matza and bitter herbs; dip parsley in salt water and horseradish in charoset; and why do we recline at the table when we eat?

AVADIM HAYINU

Folktune

The words *b'né chorin* do not appear in the liturgical text recited during the opening section of the Seder liturgy. This version, with textual modification, became popular in Israel, and then spread to Jewish communities world-wide.

A-va-dim ha-yi-nu
L'-far-o b'-mits-ra-yim
A-ta b'-né cho-rin

עֲבָדִים הָיִינוּ
לְפַרְעֹה בְּמִצְרָיִם
עַתָּה בְּנֵי חוֹרִין

Once we were slaves but now we are free men!

DAYÉNU

Folktune

Although set to a text from the Passover *Hagada*, Dayenu is one of the most popular Jewish folk melodies of the 20th century. It is sung and danced to at many joyous celebrations throughout the year.

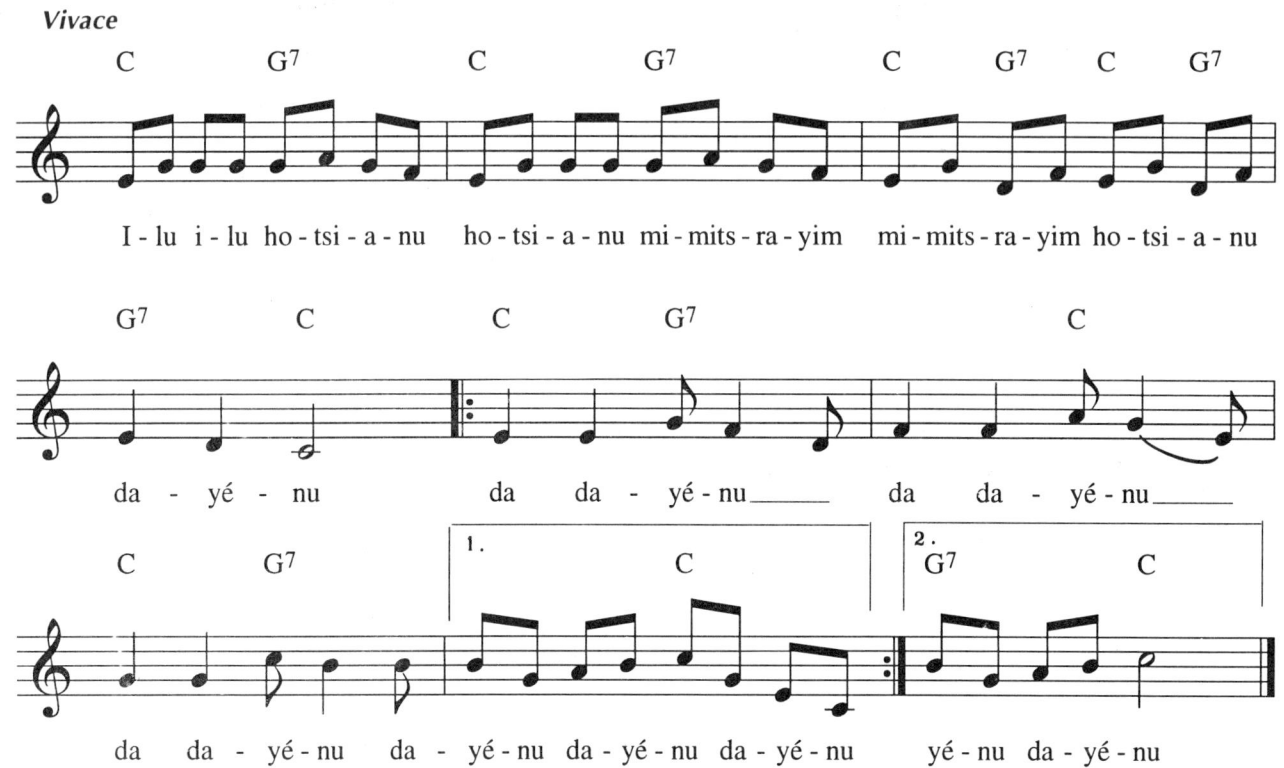

I-lu ho-tsi-a-nu mi-mits-ra-yim da-yé-nu

אִלוּ הוֹצִיאָנוּ מִמִּצְרַיִם דַּיֵּנוּ

Had He only brought us out of Egypt it would have been enough for us!

V'HI SHE'AMDA

Chassidic Folktune

V'-hi she-am-da la-a-vo-té-nu v'-la-nu
She-lo e-chad bil-vad
A-mad a-lé-nu l'-cha-lo-té-nu
E-la she-b'-chol dor va-dor
Om-dim a-lé-nu l'-cha-lo-té-nu
V'-ha-ka-dosh ba-ruch hu
Ma-tsi-lé-nu mi-ya-dam

וְהִיא שֶׁעָמְדָה לַאֲבוֹתֵינוּ וְלָנוּ
שֶׁלֹא אֶחָד בִּלְבָד
עָמַד עָלֵינוּ לְכַלוֹתֵינוּ
אֶלָא שֶׁבְּכָל דוֹר וָדוֹר
עוֹמְדִים עָלֵינוּ לְכַלוֹתֵינוּ
וְהַקָדוֹשׁ בָּרוּךְ הוּא
מַצִילֵנוּ מִיָדָם

And this is what has stood by our fathers and us. For it was not one alone who rose against us to destroy us; but in every generation there are those who rise against us to destroy us. But the Holy One, blessed is he, saves us from their hand.

CHAD GADYA

Folktune

Allegro moderato

Chad gad-ya chad gad-ya chad gad-ya chad gad-ya d'-za-bin a-ba bit-ré zu-zé chad gad-ya chad gad-ya v'-a-ta shun-ra v'-ach-la l'-gad-ya d'-za-bin a-ba bit-ré zu-zé chad gad-ya chad gad-ya

Chad gad-ya
D'-za-bin a-ba bit-ré zu-zé
Chad gad-ya
V'-at shun-ra v'-ach-la l'-gad-ya
D'-za-bin a-ba bit-ré zu-zé
Chad gad-ya

חַד גַּדְיָא חַד גַּדְיָא
דְּזַבִּין אַבָּא בִּתְרֵי זוּזֵי
חַד גַּדְיָא חַד גַּדְיָא
וְאָתָא שׁוּנְרָא וְאָכְלָה לְגַדְיָא
דְּזַבִּין אַבָּא בִּתְרֵי זוּזֵי
חַד גַּדְיָא חַד גַּדְיָא

One little goat, my father bought for two coins. Then came a cat and ate the goat my father bought for two coins.

CHAD GADYA II

Music: A. Piroznikov   Lyrics: B. Aronin

© by the authors. All rights reserved

The dog was angry with the cat
For doing such a deed
He leaped upon the frightened cat
He slew him with great speed
The stick was angry with the dog
And leaped up from his place
He beat the dog upon the head
And even on the face.   *Refrain*

The fire gave an angry roar
And leaped to the attack
It burned the stick and left it there
Like ashes crisp and black
The water came and saw the fire
It flowed all round about
It covered every single spark
And put the fire out.   *Refrain*

The thirsty ox from pasture came
And saw the water there
He drank up every single drop
Not one drop did he spare
The butcher came and saw the ox,
He firmly bound his feet
Then with his knife he slew the ox
Because he needed meat.   *Refrain*

Then came the angel dark as death
With his ten thousand eyes
He merely looked, the butcher fell,
A heap of bones he lies
Then God an angel sent to strike
The messenger of death
The angel bright blew just one puff
And slew him with his breath.   *Refrain*

ADIR HU

Folktune   Lyrics: Seder Liturgy

Adir hu yiv-ne bé-to b'-ka-rov
Bim-hé-ra b'-ya-mé-nu b'-ka-rov
El b'-né vé-t-cha b'-ka-rov

אַדִּיר הוּא יִבְנֶה בֵיתוֹ בְּקָרוֹב
בִּמְהֵרָה בְּיָמֵינוּ בְּקָרוֹב
אֵל בְּנֵה בֵיתְךָ בְּקָרוֹב

God is mighty! May he soon rebuild His Temple, speedily, in our days.

ECHAD MI YODÉ'A

Folktune   Lyrics: Seder Liturgy

Allegretto

E-chad mi yo-dé-a	אֶחָד מִי יוֹדֵעַ
E-chad a-ni yo-dé-a	אֶחָד אֲנִי יוֹדֵעַ
E-chad E-lo-hé-nu	אֶחָד אֱלֹהֵינוּ
She-ba-sha-mayim u-va-a-rets	שֶׁבַּשָּׁמַיִם וָאָרֶץ

Sh'-na-yim mi yo-dé-a	שְׁנַיִם מִי יוֹדֵעַ
Sh'-na-yim a-ni yo-dé-a	שְׁנַיִם אֲנִי יוֹדֵעַ
Sh'né lu-chot ha-brit	שְׁנֵי לֻחוֹת הַבְּרִית
E-chad Elo-hé-nu	אֶחָד אֱלֹהֵינוּ
She-ba-sha-ma-yim u-va-a-rets	שֶׁבַּשָּׁמַיִם וָאָרֶץ

Who knows one? I know one. One is our God, in heaven and on earth.
Who knows two? I know two. Two are the tablets of the covenant; One
is our God, in heaven and on earth.

L'SHANA HABA'A

L'SHANA HABA'A II

M. Nathanson

L'-sha-na ha-ba-a bi-ru-sha-la-yim

לְשָׁנָה הַבָּאָה בִּירוּשָׁלַיִם

Next year in Jerusalem!

CHASIDIC

AND

LITURGICAL

Y'VARECH'CHA

Music: D. Weinkranz Psalm: 128

A prize winning song presented at the 1970 Israeli Chassidic Song Festival. *Y'varech'cha* has proved its staying power and is still very popular today.

Y'-va-re-ch'-cha Ha-shem mi-tsi-yon
Ur'-é b'-tuv Y'-ru-sha-la-yim
Kol y'-mé cha-ye-cha
Ur'-é va-nim l'-va-ne-cha
Sha-lom al Yis-ra-él

יְבָרֶכְךָ ה' מִצִּיּוֹן
וּרְאֵה בְּטוּב יְרוּשָׁלַיִם
כָּל יְמֵי חַיֶּיךָ
וּרְאֵה בָנִים לְבָנֶיךָ
שָׁלוֹם עַל יִשְׂרָאֵל

The Lord bless you from Zion; may you see the welfare of Jerusalem all the days of your life; may you live to see your children's children. Peace be upon Israel.

BILVAVI

S. Brazil   Lyrics: Sefer Charedim

Bil-va-vi mish-kan ev-ne l'-ha-dar k'-vo-do
U-v'-mish-kan miz-bé-ach a-sim l'-kar-né ho-do
U-l'-nér ta-mid e-kach li et ésh ha-a-ké-da
U-l'-kor-ban ak-riv lo et naf-shi et naf-shi ha-y'-chi-da

בִּלְבָבִי מִשְׁכָּן אֶבְנֶה לְהַדַר כְּבוֹדוֹ
וּבְמִשְׁכָּן מִזְבֵּחַ אָשִׂים לְקַרְנֵי הוֹדוֹ
וּלְנֵר תָּמִיד אֶקַּח לִי אֶת אֵשׁ הָעֲקֵדָה
וּלְקָרְבָּן אַקְרִיב לוֹ אֶת נַפְשִׁי הַיְחִידָה

In my heart I will erect a sanctuary to glorify His honor. In the sanctuary I will place an altar to acknowledge His splendor. For the eternal light I will take the fire of Isaac's binding and with this my singular soul, will I sacrifice before him.

TSIYON

Traditional

This well known folktune has been adopted by the Japanese Christian group *Makuya* as its theme song. Many *Makuya* students spend a year in Israel in a kibbutz or at a university. In addition, they take on Hebrew names, speak the language and present Israeli music programs to many international touring groups.

Moderately

Tsi-yon ha-lo tish-a-li
Lish-lom a-si-ra-yich

צִיּוֹן הֲלֹא תִּשְׁאֲלִי
לִשְׁלוֹם אֲסִירַיִךְ

O Zion why are you not concerned with the welfare of your prisoners?

214

ZARA

Music: Hassidic   Lyrics: Liturgy

Zar-a cha-ya v'-ka-ya-ma
Zar-a di lo yif-suk
V'-di lo yiv-tul
Mi pit-ga-mé o-rai-ta

זַרְעָא חַיָּא וְקַיָּמָא
זַרְעָא דִי לָא יִפְסֵק
וְדִי לָא יִבְטֵל
מִפִּתְגָּמֵי אוֹרַיְתָא

May we be granted healthy children who will never neglect the study of Torah.

ESA ÉNAI

S. Carlebach   Lyrics: Psalm 121: 1

©by the Author. All rights reserved

E-sa é-nai el he-ha-rim
Mé-a-yin ya-vo ez-ri
Ez-ri mé-im Ha-shem
O-sé sha-ma-yim va-a-rets

אֶשָּׂא עֵינַי אֶל הֶהָרִים
מֵאַיִן יָבוֹא עֶזְרִי
עֶזְרִי מֵעִם יְיָ
עוֹשֵׂה שָׁמַיִם וָאָרֶץ

I lift up my eyes to the hills. Whence comes my help? My help is from the Lord, Creator of heaven and earth.

MOSHE EMET

Hassidic

Moshe e-met v'-to-ra-to e-met

מֹשֶׁה אֱמֶת וְתוֹרָתוֹ אֱמֶת

Moses and the Tora are true and genuine!

ÉLE CHAMDA LIBI

Music: Hassidic   Lyrics: Liturgy

Allegro moderato

É - le cham - da li - bi v' - chu - sa na v' - al tit - a - lém
é - le cham - da cham - da li - bi v' - chu - sa na v' - al tit - a - lém
lém é - le cham - da li - bi v' - chu - sa na v' - al tit - a - lém
é - le cham - da cham - da li - bi v' - chu - sa na v' - al tit - a - lém lém

É-le cham-da li-bi
V'-chu-sa na v'-al tit-a-lém

אֵלֶה חָמְדָה לִבִּי
וְחוּסָה נָא וְאַל תִּתְעַלֵּם

These are the desires of my heart. Have mercy and turn not away from us.

AVINU MALKÉNU

This text is recited on fast days during the Ten Days of Penitence and before the end of the Yom Kippur service.

Folktune   Lyrics: Liturgy

A-vi-nu mal-ké-nu
Cha-né-nu va-a-né-nu
Ki én ba-nu ma-a-sim
A-sé i-ma-nu
Ts'-da-ka va-che-sed
V'-ho-shi-é-nu

אָבִינוּ מַלְכֵּנוּ
חָנֵּנוּ וַעֲנֵנוּ
כִּי אֵין בָּנוּ מַעֲשִׂים
עֲשֵׂה עִמָּנוּ
צְדָקָה וָחֶסֶד
וְהוֹשִׁיעֵנוּ

Our Father, our King, be gracious unto us and answer us, for we are unworthy; deal with us in charity and lovingkindness and save us.

KOL HA'OLAM KULO

B. Chait   Lyrics: Rabbi Nachman of Bratslav

©by the Author. All rights reserved

Kol ha-o-lam ku-lo ge-sher tsar m'-od
V'-ha-i-kar lo l'fa-chéd k'lal

כָּל הָעוֹלָם כֻּלּוֹ גֶּשֶׁר צַר מְאֹד
וְהָעִיקָר לֹא לְפַחֵד כְּלָל

The entire world is a narrow bridge. But the main thing is not to fear.

V'HA'ÉR ÉNÉNU

S. Carlebach   Lyrics: Liturgy

This melody by Rabbi Shlomo Carlebach, was introduced in Israel via the first Hassidic Song Festival in 1969. Rabbi Carlebach's songs appeared in each successive festival and gained wide popularity. Although Israelis had not previously adopted melodies set to liturgical texts as national popular songs, *V'haer Enenu* became an overnight runaway "hit".

©by the Author. All rights reserved

V'-ha-ér é-né-nu b'-to-ra-te-cha
V'-da-bék li-bé-nu b'-mits-vo-te-cha
V'-ya-chéd l'-va-vé-nu l'-a-ha-va
U-l'-yir-a et sh'-me-cha
She-lo né-vosh v'-lo ni-ka-lém
V'-lo ni-ka-shél l'-o-lam va-ed

וְהָאֵר עֵינֵינוּ בְּתוֹרָתֶךָ
וְדַבֵּק לִבֵּנוּ בְּמִצְוֹתֶיךָ
וְיַחֵד לְבָבֵנוּ לְאַהֲבָה
וּלְיִרְאָה אֶת שְׁמֶךָ
שֶׁלֹא נֵבוֹשׁ וְלֹא נִכָּלֵם
וְלֹא נִכָּשֵׁל לְעוֹלָם וָעֶד

Enlighten our eyes to your Torah; attach our heart to Your commandments.
Unite our heart to love and revere Your name so that we may never be put to shame.

SHALOM RAV

Music: D. Freelander & J. Klepper Lyrics: Liturgy

Shalom Rav has become a "classic" in the NFTY (National Federation of Temple Youth) organization as well as in educational institutions, summer camps and Havurot.

222

Sha-lom rav al Yis-ra-él am-cha
Ta-sim l'-o-lam
Ki a-ta hu me-lech a-don
L'chol ha-sha-lom
V'tov b'-é-ne-cha l'-va-réch
Et am-cha Yis-ra-él
B'-chol ét u-v'-chol sha-a
Bish-lo-me-cha

שָׁלוֹם רַב עַל יִשְׂרָאֵל עַמְּךָ
תָּשִׂים לְעוֹלָם
כִּי אַתָּה הוּא מֶלֶךְ אָדוֹן
לְכָל הַשָּׁלוֹם
וְטוֹב בְּעֵינֶיךָ לְבָרֵךְ
אֶת עַמְּךָ יִשְׂרָאֵל
בְּכָל עֵת וּבְכָל שָׁעָה
בִּשְׁלוֹמֶךָ

O grant abundant peace to Israel your people forever, for You are the King and Lord of peace. May it please You to bless us and to bless all Your people Israel with your peace at all times and at all hours.

SHEYIBANE BET HAMIKDASH

This is the closing section of a well known cantorial composition by Israel Schorr. It became closely associated with Moshe Koussevitsky, one of the premiere cantors of the 20th century.

Music: I. Schorr   Lyrics: Liturgy

She-yi-ba-ne bét ha-mik-dash
Bim-hé-ra v'-ya-mé-nu
V'-tén chel-ké-nu b'to-ra-te-cha

שֶׁיִּבָּנֶה בֵּית הַמִּקְדָּשׁ
בִּמְהֵרָה בְיָמֵינוּ
וְתֵן חֶלְקֵנוּ בְּתוֹרָתֶךָ

May the Temple be speedily rebuilt in our days, and grant us a share in your Tora.

YISM'CHU HASHAMAYIM

Music: Hassidic   Lyrics: Liturgy

The melody composed by the Rebbe of Pittsburgh has become a well-known song throughout the Jewish community world-wide.

Yis-m'-chu ha-sha-ma-yim
V'-ta-gél ha-a-rets
Yir-am ha-yam u-m'lo-o

יִשְׂמְחוּ הַשָּׁמַיִם
וְתָגֵל הָאָרֶץ
יִרְעַם הַיָּם וּמְלֹאוֹ

Let the heavens rejoice and let the earth be glad.
Let the sea roar and the fullness thereof.

KI MITSIYON

Music: N. Shachar   Lyrics: Liturgy

Ki mi-tsi-yon té-tsé To-ra
Ud-var Ha-shem mi-ru-sha-la-yim
Ba-ruch she-na-tan To-ra
L'-a-mo Yis-ra-él bik-du-sha-to

כִּי מִצִּיוֹן תֵּצֵא תוֹרָה
וּדְבַר יְיָ מִירוּשָׁלָיִם
בָּרוּךְ שֶׁנָּתַן תּוֹרָה
לְעַמּוֹ יִשְׂרָאֵל בִּקְדֻשָּׁתוֹ

Truly out of Zion shall come forth the Tora, and the word of the Lord out of Jerusalem:

ÉTS CHAYIM HI

Music: T. Portnoy   Lyrics: Liturgy

ti - vo - te ha sha - lom_____

©by the Author. All rights reserved

Ki le-kach tov na-ta-ti la-chem
To-ra-ti al ta-a-zo-vu
Ets cha-yim hi la-ma-cha-zi-kim ba
V'-tom-che-ha m'-u-shar
D'-ra-che-ha dar-ché no-am
V'-chol n'-ti-vo-te-ha sha-lom

כִּי לֶקַח טוֹב נָתַתִּי לָכֶם
תּוֹרָתִי אַל תַּעֲזֹבוּ
עֵץ חַיִּים הִיא לַמַּחֲזִיקִים בָּהּ
וְתֹמְכֶיהָ מְאֻשָּׁר
דְּרָכֶיהָ דַרְכֵי נֹעַם
וְכָל נְתִיבוֹתֶיהָ שָׁלוֹם

It is a tree of life to those who take hold of it, and happy are those who support it. Its ways are the ways of pleasantness, and all its paths are peace. Turn us to you, O Lord, and let us return; renew our days as of old.

UVA'U HA'OVDIM

S. Carlebach   Lyrics: Isaiah 27: 13

©by the Author. All rights reserved

U-va-u ha-ov-dim b'-e-rets a-shur
V'-ha-ni-da-chim b'-e-rets mits-ra-yim
V'-hish-ta-cha-vu la-shem b'-har ha-ko-desh
Bi-ru-sha-la-yim

וּבָאוּ הָאֹבְדִים בְּאֶרֶץ אַשּׁוּר
וְהַנִּדָּחִים בְּאֶרֶץ מִצְרָיִם
וְהִשְׁתַּחֲווּ לַיְיָ בְּהַר הַקֹּדֶשׁ
בִּירוּשָׁלָיִם

And they shall come that were lost in the land of Assyria, and they that were dispersed in the land of Egypt; and they shall worship the Lord in the holy mountain at Jerusalem.

SIMAN TOV

This is the traditional Mazel Tov (good luck) song played and sung at happy occasions in Jewish life.

Traditional

Si-man tov u-ma-zl tov
Y'hé la-nu u-l'chol Yis-ra-él

סִימָן טוֹב וּמַזָּל טוֹב
יְהֵא לָנוּ וּלְכָל יִשְׂרָאֵל

May good fortune come to us and to all Israel.

OD YISHAMA

Traditional   Lyrics: Wedding Benedictions

This melody to the text of one of the "Seven Wedding Benedictions," is used during the *Badeken* (veiling of the bride) ceremony as well as the wedding recessional.

Od yi-sha-ma b'a-ré Y'hu-da
Uv'-chu-tsot Y'-ru-sha-la-yim
Kol sa-son v'-kol sim-cha
Kol cha-tan v'-kol ka-la

עוֹד יִשָּׁמַע בְּעָרֵי יְהוּדָה
וּבְחוּצוֹת יְרוּשָׁלָיִם
קוֹל שָׂשׂוֹן וְקוֹל שִׂמְחָה
קוֹל חָתָן וְקוֹל כַּלָּה

Again may there be heard in the cities of Judah and the streets of Jerusalem the voice of gladness, the voice of bridegroom and bride.

OD YISHAMA II

S. Carlebach

©by the Author. All rights reserved

Od yi-sha-ma b'-a-ré Y'-hu-da
Uv'-chu-tsot Y'-ru-sha-la-yim
Kol sa-son v'-kol sim-cha
Kol cha-tan v'-kol ka-la

עוֹד יִשָּׁמַע בְּעָרֵי יְהוּדָה
וּבְחוּצוֹת יְרוּשָׁלַיִם
קוֹל שָׂשׂוֹן וְקוֹל שִׂמְחָה
קוֹל חָתָן וְקוֹל כַּלָה

Again may there be heard in the cities of Judah and in the streets of Jerusalem the voice of gladness, the voice of bridegroom and bride.

SHEHECHEYANU

Music: Z. Pick   Lyrics: Liturgy

Zvicka Pick's melody was presented at an Israel Chassidic Song Festival. It became a favorite in Israel as well as the United States.

234

she - he - che - ya - nu v' - ki - ma - nu   v' - hi - gi - a - nu laz - man ha - ze

©by the Author. All rights reserved

Ba-ruch a-ta Ha-shem E-lo-ké-nu
Me-lech ha-o-lam
She-he-che-ya-nu v'-ki-ma-nu
V'-hi-gi-a-nu laz-man ha-ze

בָּרוּךְ אַתָּה יְיָ אֱלֹהֵינוּ
מֶלֶךְ הָעוֹלָם
שֶׁהֶחֱיָנוּ וְקִיְּמָנוּ
וְהִגִּיעָנוּ לַזְּמַן הַזֶּה

Blessed art Thou, O Lord our God, King of the universe, who has given us life and brought us to this season.

BIRKAT HAMAZON

Music: M. Nathanson   Lyrics: Liturgy

This well-known melodic setting for the first section of the *Grace After Meals* is often thought of as a folktune. It was composed by Moshe Nathanson a cantor, music teacher and composer. Nathanson also wrote the lyrics for Hava Nagila (see note page 34.)

Moderately

Ba - ruch a - ta___ A - do - nai E - lo -
hé - nu me - lech ha - o - lam___ ha - zan et ha - o - lam ku -
lo b' - tu - vo b' - chén b' - che - sed uv - ra - cha - mim___
hu no - tén le - chem l' - chol ba - sar ki l' - o - lam chas -
do___ uv - tu - vo ha - ga - dol___ ta - mid lo cha - sar la - nu
v' - al yech - sar la - nu ma - zon l' - o - lam va - ed ba - a -
vur sh' - a - mo ha - ga - dol___ ki hu Él zan um - far - nés la -

Ba-ruch a-ta A-do-nai	בָּרוּךְ אַתָּה יְיָ
E-lo-hénu me-lech ha-o-lam	אֱלֹהֵינוּ מֶלֶךְ הָעוֹלָם
Ha-zan et ha-o-lam ku-lo b'-tu-vo	הַזָּן אֶת הָעוֹלָם כֻּלּוֹ בְּטוּבוֹ
B'-chén b'-che-sed uv-ra-cha-mim	בְּחֵן בְּחֶסֶד וּבְרַחֲמִים
Hu no-tén le-chem l'-chol ba-sar	הוּא נוֹתֵן לֶחֶם לְכָל בָּשָׂר
Ki l'-o-lam chas-do	כִּי לְעוֹלָם חַסְדּוֹ
Uv-tu-vo ha-ga-dol	וּבְטוּבוֹ הַגָּדוֹל
Ta-mid lo cha-sar la-nu	תָּמִיד לֹא חָסַר לָנוּ
V'-al yech-sar la-nu	וְאַל יֶחְסַר לָנוּ
Ma-zon l'-o-lam va-ed	מָזוֹן לְעוֹלָם וָעֶד
Ba-a-vur sh'-mo ha-ga-dol	בַּעֲבוּר שְׁמוֹ הַגָּדוֹל
Ki hu Él zan um-far-nés la-kol	כִּי הוּא אֵל זָן וּמְפַרְנֵס לַכֹּל
U-mé-tiv la-kol u-mé-chin ma-zon	וּמֵטִיב לַכֹּל וּמֵכִין מָזוֹן
L'-chol b'-ri-o-tav a-sher ba-ra	לְכָל בְּרִיּוֹתָיו אֲשֶׁר בָּרָא
Ba-ruch a-ta A-do-nai	בָּרוּךְ אַתָּה יְיָ
Ha-zan et ha-kol	הַזָּן אֶת הַכֹּל

Blessed are You, God, King of the universe who sustains the whole world in His goodness, grace, mercy and compassion, giving bread to all flesh. And through Your great goodness food has never been wanting for us, nor will it ever be wanting for us. Blessed are You who feeds all.

MITSVA G'DOLA
Hassidic

Mits-va g'-do-la li-yot b'-sim-cha ta-mid

מִצְוָה גְדוֹלָה לִהְיוֹת בְּשִׂמְחָה תָּמִיד

It is a great *mitsva* to be joyful.

ANI MA'AMIN

Music: A.D. Fastag   Lyrics: Liturgy

Lyrics: Maimonides, 12th Principle of Faith

Ani Ma'amin has become one of the best known songs to emerge from the Warsaw Ghetto. It was composed by the Hassidic (Modzitz) singer-composer Azriel Dovid Fastag. According to documentation, thousands of Jews sang this melody to the text of "I Believe" (from Maimonides' Thirteen Articles of Faith) as they marched to their deaths in the gas chambers.

A-ni ma-a-min be-e-mu-na sh'-lé-ma
B'-vi-at ha-ma-shi-ach
V'-af al pi she-yit-ma-mé-ha
Im kol ze a-ni ma-a-min

אֲנִי מַאֲמִין בֶּאֱמוּנָה שְׁלֵמָה
בְּבִיאַת הַמָּשִׁיחַ
וְאַף עַל פִּי שֶׁיִּתְמַהְמֵהַּ
עִם כָּל זֶה אֲנִי מַאֲמִין

I believe with perfect faith in the coming of the Messiah; and although he may tarry, I believe.

ÉLI ATA

Hassidic

One of the ten "holy" songs of the *Chabad* chassidim attributed to Rabbiu Shneur Zalman of Liadi, the first Rebe of Lubavitch.

Eli Ata v'-o-de-ka E-lo-hai a-ro-m'-me-ka

אֵלִי אַתָּה וְאוֹדֶךָּ אֱלֹהַי אֲרוֹמְמֶךָ

You are my God and I will give thanks to You.
You are my God and I will exult You.

SAMCHÉM

Music: M. Laufer   Lyrics: Liturgy

Sam-chém b'-vin-yan sha-lém

שַׂמְּחֵם בְּבִנְיַן שָׁלֵם

Gladden them with rebuilt Jerusalem.

MASHIACH

M. Laufer & M. Ben David
Lyrics: Maimonides, 12th principle of faith

A-ni ma-a-min be-e-mu-na sh'-lé-ma
B'-vi-at ha-ma-shi-ach
V'-af al pi she-yit-ma-mé-ha
Im kol ze a-ni ma-a-min

אֲנִי מַאֲמִין בֶּאֱמוּנָה שְׁלֵמָה
בְּבִיאַת הַמָּשִׁיחַ
וְאַף עַל פִּי שֶׁיִּתְמַהְמֵהַּ
עִם כָּל זֶה אֲחַכֶּה לוֹ
בְּכָל יוֹם שֶׁיָּבוֹא

I believe with perfect faith in the coming of the Messiah; and although he may tarry, I believe.

NYE ZU RITSE CHLOPTSI

Russian Folksong

This song, a favorite of the Lubavitcher Chasidim, has been taken over in the original Russian language from the peasant repertoire. During the time of the *Mitler Rebe*, Rabbi Duber, it was sung by the Chasidim as they journeyed to and from Lubavitch. For the Chasidim, it has a deeper meaning than is evident from the literal translation. According to them, the song offers Jewish consolation in proclaiming that God on high will provide for all their material needs.

Nye zu-ritse chlop-tsi shto s'-nami bud-yet
Mi po-ye-dem na kar-tshon-ki tam i vodka bud-yet

Don't worry fellows about what will become of us. We will travel to an inn where there will surely be vodka to drink.

SHMELKIE'S NIGUN

S. Brazil

©by the Author. All rights reserved

NIGUN

Attributed to the chassidim of Bobov, this melody is often used as a processional during the traditional Jewish wedding ceremony.

Hassidic

NIGUN

Hassidic

In the late 1960s a musical play, *Ish Chasid Haya* (Once there was a Chasid) was staged in Tel Aviv. The chassidic *nigun* (wordless song) presented here, was a featured melody and soon became a favorite in Jewish communities around the world.

NIGUN

Hassidic

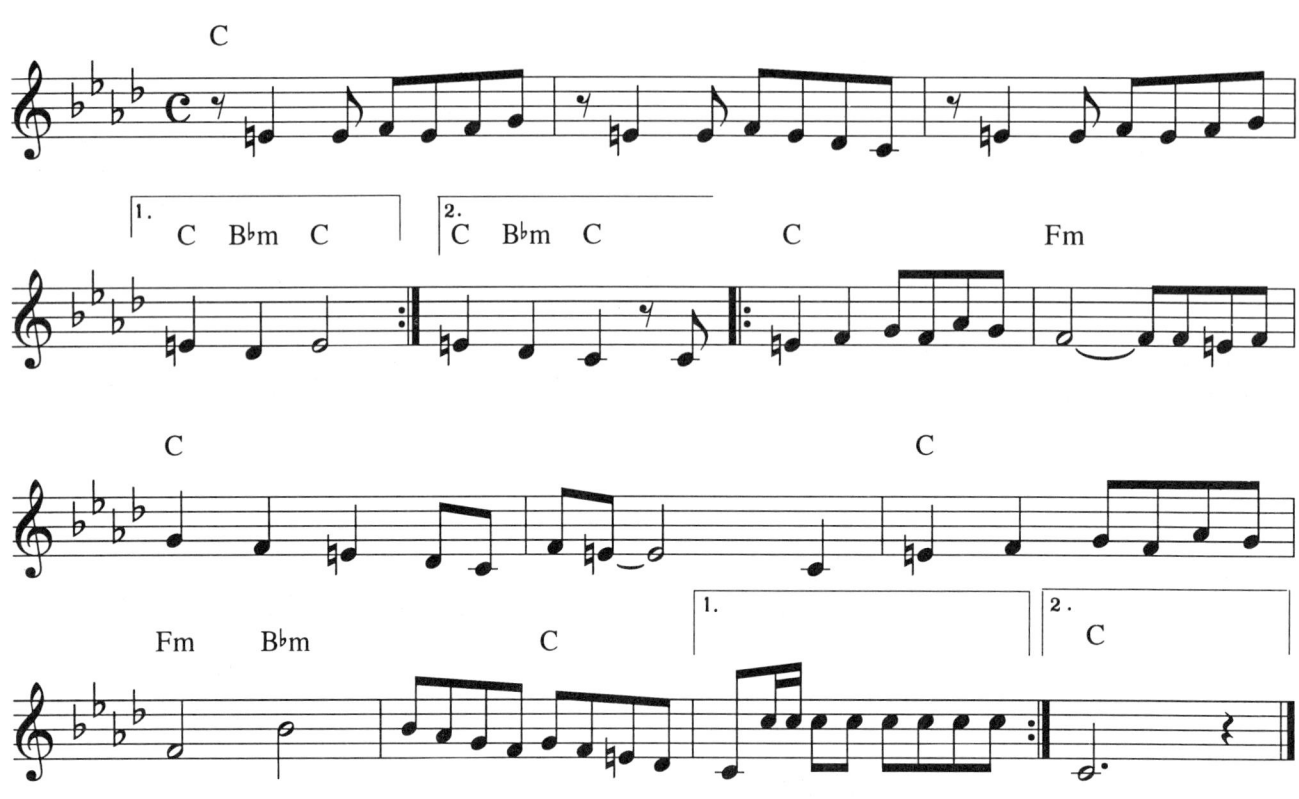

NIGUN

Hassidic

SELECTED BIBLIOGRAPHY

SONGS OF ISRAEL
A Harvest Of Jewish Song, ed. V. Pasternak, Tara Publications, Cedarhurst, N.Y. 1980
Favorite Songs of Israel, ed. V. Pasternak, Tara Publications, Cedarhurst, N.Y. 1985
Great Songs of Israel, ed. V. Pasternak, Tara Publications, Cedarhurst, N.Y. 1976
Israel In Song, ed. V. Pasternak, Tara Publications, Cedarhurst, N.Y. 1974
L'yisrael Mizmor, ed. C. Goldberg, BJE, N.Y. 1988
The Israeli Pops Songbook, ed. V. Pasternak, Tara Publications, Cedarhurst, N.Y. 1989

SONGS IN YIDDISH
Great Jewish Classics Vols1-7, Tara Publications, Cedarhurst, N.Y. 1981-1992
Great Songs of the Yiddish Theater, ed. N. Warembud, J&J Kammen, N.Y. 1975
Jewish Nostalgia, J & J Kammen, N.Y. 1970
Mir Trogn A Gezang, ed. E. Mlotek, Workmen's Circle, N.Y. 1989
Most Popular Jewish Songs, J&J Kammen, N.Y. 1960
Pearls of Yiddish, ed. C and J. Mlotek, Workmen's Circle, N.Y. 1982

SEPHARDIC AND ORIENTAL
Sephardic Songs of Praise, A. Cardozo, Tara Publications, Cedarhurst, 1989
The Flory Jagoda Songbook, Tara Publications, Cedarhurst, N.Y. 1993
The Ladino Songbook, ed. N. Castel, Tara Publications, Cedarhurst, N.Y. 1981
The Sephardic-Oriental Songbook, ed. V. Pasternak, Tara Publications, Cedarhurst, N.Y. 1989

SONGS IN ENGLISH
NFTY in Harmony, ed. R. and M. Arian, Tara Publications, Cedarhurst, N.Y. 1991
The Best of Debbie Friedman, Tara Publications, Cedarhurst, N.Y. 1987

SABBATH AND HOLIDAYS
Holidays in Song, ed. V. Pasternak, Tara Publications, Cedarhurst, N.Y. 1985
The Harvard Hillel Songbook, D. Godine, Boston, Ma. 1992
The Z'mirot Anthology, ed. N. Levin, Tara Publications, Cedarhurst, N.Y. 1981

HASSIDIC & LITURGICAL
Siddur in Song, ed. V. Pasternak, Tara Publications, Cedarhurst, N.Y. 1986
The Best Of Hassidic Song, ed. V. Pasternak, Tara Publications, Cedarhurst, N.Y. 1984
The Best of the Chassidic Song Festivals, ed. V. Pasternak, Tara Publications, Cedarhurst, N.Y. 1989
The Shlomo Carlebach Anthology, Tara Publications, Cedarhurst, N.Y. 1993
Songs of Joy, ed. V. Pasternak, Tara Publications, Cedarhurst, N.Y. 1993

INDEX OF FIRST LINES

A kalte nacht a nepldike /88
A shvester bin ich dir a trai'e /108
Adir hu yivne véto b'karov /208
Adon olam asher malach /176, 178
Al hadvash v'al ha'oketz /48
Am Yisrael chai od avinu chai /10
Amda na'ara mul hakotel /44
Amén shém nora /151
An emese éshes chayil /84
Ani ma'amin be'emuna sh'léma /239
Ani nolad'ti el hamanginot /62
Ani Purim samé'ach umvadé'ach /198
Artsa alinu k'var charashnu /22
As I watch you light the Sabbath candles /156
Avadim hayinu ata b'né chorin /203
Avinu malkénu chanénu va'anénu /219
Avir harim tsalul kayayin v'ré'ach oranim /56
Az der rebe Elimelech iz gevoren /76
Az ich vel zingen l'cha dodi /112
Az yashir Moshe uv'né Yisraél /149
B'arvot hanegev mitnotsét hatal /14
B'éle hayadayim od lo baniti k'far /30
B'shem kol hatankistim ufnéhem ham'uvakot /52
Bashana haba'a néshev al hamirpeset /32
Belz main shtétele Belz /98
Bilvavi mishkan evne /213
Chad Gadya d'zabin aba bitré zuzé /206
Chag Purim chag gadol hu lay'hudim /199
Chanuka chag yafe kol kach /195
Chosn kale mazel tov /115
Cuando el rey nimrod al campo sali'a /122
D'ror yikra l'vén im bat /143
David Melech Yisraél chai v'kayam /11
Der Yid vert geyogt un geplogt /104
Dodi li va-ani lo ha-ro'e ba-sho-shanim /19
Durme ijiko de madre /128
Echad mi yodé'a /209
El ginat egoz yarad'ti /46
Ele chamda libi v'chusa na v'al titalém /218
Eli ata v'odeka Elohai arom'meka /240

Eli Eli lama azavtáni /78
Eli Eli shelo yigamér l'olam /31
Eliyahu hanavi Eliyahu hatishbi /187
En adir ka-donai v'én baruch k'ven am'ram /152
En kelohénu én kadonénu /150
Erev shel shoshanim nétsé na el habustan /37
Es iz tsu mir gekumen a kuzine /92
Esa énai el heharim mé'ayin yavo ezri /216
Eshet chayil mi yimtsa /181
Ets chayim hi lamachazikim ba /228
Ets harimon natan récho /139
Gizratéch tavnit noga /130
Ha lachma anya di achalu avhatana /200
Hachama mérosh ha'ilanot nistalka 172
Hal'luya la'olam hal'luya yashiru kulam /58
Hamavdil bén kodesh l'chol /153
Hanuka linda staki /132
Haru'ach noshevet k'rira /36
Hashkédiya porachat /197
Hava nagila v'nism'cha /34
Hazan et ha'olam kulo b'tuvo /236
Hecher beser di rod macht greser /114
Hevenu shalom alechem /11
Hiné ba b'hod tokfo /194
Hiné ma tov uma na'im /24, 25
Hu hayoshev lo é sham bamromim /38
I am the sun Jerusalem /160
I have a little dreydl /196
Ich vil bai aich a kashe frégn /85
Ilu hotsi'anu mimitsrayim dayénu /204
Im bahar chatsavta even /26
Im yésh é sham rachok /129
In dem Bés Hamikdosh in a vinkel chéder /74
K'she'ima ba'a héna yafa uts'ira /12
K'var acharé chatsot /27
Kadésh urchats karpas yachats /146, 147
Ki eshm'ra Shabat El yishm'réni /141
Ki mitsiyon tétse tora /227
Kol ha'olam kulo gesher tsar m'od /220
Kol od balévav p'nima /68

L'cha dodi likrat kala / 174, 175
L'chi lach to a land that I will show you /242
L'hadlik nér shel chanuka /189
L'shana haba'a birushalayim /210
Lach Y'rushalayim bén chomot ha'ir /54
Lanér v'livsamim nafshi m'yachéla /133
Let's learn the Alef Bet /170
Light one candle for the Maccabee children /166
Lo yisa goi el goi cherev /70
Los bilbilicos cantan consos piros de amor /123
M'chuténiste maine m'chuténiste getraye /93
Ma avaréch lo bame y'vorach /47
Ma nishtana halaila haze /201, 202
Ma'oz tsur y'shu'ati /145, 190
Machar ulai nafliga basfinot /50
Main chai'es gét mir ois /116
Main kind main trést du forst avek /96
Mé'al pisgat har hatsofim /64
Mi y'malel g'vurot Yisraél /191
Misaviv yéhom hasa'ar /28
Mitsva g'dola liyot b'simcha tamid /238
Mizmor l'david havu ladonai /134, 136
Moshe emet v'torato emet /217
My Zédi lived with us /168
Na'ara tova y'fat énayim lanu yésh b'erets /20
Nye zu ritse chloptsi /242
O grandpa went to market once 207
Od nashuva el nigun atik /40
Od yésh mifras lavan ba'ofek /14
Od yishama b'aré Y'huda /232, 233
Oifn pripitchik brent a fayerl /72
On a wagon bound for market /162
Ongezolyet oifn hartsen /110
Or vat'chélet bashamayim /35
Ose shalom Bimromav /9
Quen supiese y entendiense /148
Rad halaila rav shirénu /42
Rumania geven a mol a land /118
S'brent briderlech s'brent /106
S'vivon sov sov sov /192

Samchém b'vinyan shalem /241
Scalerica de oro y de marfil /124
Shabat shalom /179
Shalom aléchem malaché hasharét /180
Shalom rav al Yisraél /222
Sheheicheyanu v'kimanu v'higi'anu /234
Shén vi di l'vone lichtig vi di shtern /102
Sheyibane bét hamikdash /225
Shimu achai ani od chai /60
Shir hama'alot b'shuv Adonai /185, 186
Shlof zhe mir shoin Yankele /90
Shtét a bochur un er tracht /94
Shtét zich dort in gesele /100
Shuv ha'eder nohér bimvo'ot hakfar /23
Siman tov umazal tov y'hé lanu /231
Sisu et Y'rushalayim gilu va /66
Sisu v'simchu b'simchat Tora /188
They called me Anatole in prison I did lie /158
Tsena habanot ur'ena /41
Tsiyon halo tishali lishlom asirayich /214
Tsur mishelo achalnu bar'chu emunai /184
Ufaratsta yama vakédma /224
Un az der rebe zingt /80
Ush'avtem mayim b'sason /18
Uva'u ha'ovdim b'erets ashur /230
V'ha'ér énénu b'toratecha /221
V'hi she'amda lavoténu v'lanu /205
Ven di zolst zain shvartz vi a tuter /81
Y'did nefesh av harachaman /173
Y'mé hachanuka chanukat mikdashénu /193
Y'varech'cha Hashem mitsiyon /212
Ya ribon alam v'almaya /183
Yigdal Elohim chai v'yishtabach /145
Yism'chu hashamayim v'tagél ha'arets /226
Yitsmach shalom rav mé'artsi /138
Yo m'enamori d'un aire /126
Yom ze l'yisraél ora v'simcha /140
Yome Yome shpil mir a lidele /101
Zara chaya v'kayama /215
Zog nit kénmol az du gést dem letsten veg /107

SELECTED DISCOGRAPHY

A Israel's Greatest Hits — *CBS 40-65305*
B The Very Best of Israel — *NMC-460815*
C Israel's Greatest Songs— *CBS 25309*
D Sefarad— *Tara PublicationsTR590*
E Toast To Life— *Tara Publications— TR609*
F Seder Melodies— *Tara Publications*
G Happy Chanukah!— *Mint Productions*
H Sabbath Songs in the Sephardic Tradition—*CBS 82760*
I Theodore Bikel Sings Jewish Folksongs— *Bainbridge 2507*
J Theodore Bikel Sings More Jewish Folksongs— *Bainbridge 2508*
K Theodore Bikel Sings Yiddish Theater— *Bainbridge 2504*
L The Yiddish Dream—*Omega OVC6004*
M Z'mirot-Sabbath Songs For The Home— *Tara Publications*
N Sephardic Songs of Praise— *Tara Publications SSP101*
O Life's a Lesson— *Go Jazz 53701*
P Hava Nagila— *CBS 69029*
Q Safam's Greatest Hits— *Safam SFM008*
R Songs For Hanukah and Other Festivals— *Haimsche Music*
S 20 Chassidic Songs— *Koliphone 7474*
T Chassidic Hits Compilation Vol. 2— *Helicon 35437*
U Kantikas Di Mi Nona—*Global Village C139*
V Jan Peerce Sings Hebrew Melodies— *Israel Music IMC1010*
W The Barry Sisters Greatest Hits—*Tradition 2213*
X Mazel Tov—*Tara Publications ZS800*
Y Holidays in the Sephardic Heritage—*CP Music*
Z Connie Frances Sings Yiddish Songs—*Leisure Time Records CPSM 5085*

Adir Hu **F**	Erev Ba **A**	Od Yishama II **X**
Adon Olam **P**	Erev Shel Shoshanim **B**	Oifn Pripitchik **L**
Adon Olam **T**	Ha Lachma **F**	Quen Su Piese **Y**
Al Kol Elé **Q**	Hafinjan **P**	Rézele **L**
Am Yisrael Chai **X**	Hal'luya **C**	Rozhinkes Mit Mandlen **L**
Amen Shém Nora **N**	Halicha L'késaria **O**	S'vivon **G**
Avadim Hayinu **F**	Hamavdil **H**	Samchém **T**
Avinu Malkénu **O**	Hatikva **B**	Scalerica D'oro **D**
Az Der Rebbe Zingt **J**	Hava Nagila **A**	Shalom Aléchem **R**
Az Yashir Moshe **N**	Hiné Ma Tov **X**	Shein Vi Di L'vone **Z**
Bashana Haba-a **A**	Hitragut **X**	Siman Tov **S**
Nigun-Ai Di Di Di **S**	I Have a Little Dredl **G**	Sisu Et Y'rushalayim **B**
Birkat Hamazon **M**	Jerusalem of Gold **B**	Tsena **B**
Brivele Der Mamen **E**	K'var Acharé Chatso **X**	Tumbalalaika **I**
Chad Gadya **F**	Kadésh Urchats **F**	Ufaratsta **S**
Chad Gadya **F**	L'cha Dodi **A**	Uvau Ha-ovdim **T**
Chanuka Blessings **G**	L'shana Haba'a II **F**	V'haér Enénu **A**
Chanuka Chag Yafe **G**	Leaving Mother Russia **Q**	V'hi She'amda **F**
Chiribim **L**	Los Bilbilicos **D**	Vu Ahin Zol Ich Gén **W**
Chorshat Ha-ekaliptus **A**	Ma Nishtana II **F**	Y'did Nefesh **O**
Cuando El Rey Nimrod **D**	Ma'oz Tsur **G**	Y'mé Hachanuka **G**
D'ror Yikra **H**	Ma'oz Tzur **G**	Ya Ribon **M**
David Melech Yisraél **A**	Machar **A**	Yiddishe Momme **Z**
Dayénu **R**	Mayim, Mayim **X**	Yigdal **N**
Der Rebbe Elimelech **E**	M'chutenjsta **K**	Yism'chu Hashamayim **S**
Di Greene Kuzine **K**	Mein Shtetele Belz **K**	Yo M'enamori D'un Aire **D**
Di Mezinke **I**	Mi Pi El **Y**	Yome Yome **L**
Dodi Li **X**	Mi Y'malél **G**	Zemer Atik **X**
Donna Donna **J**	Mizmor L'david **H**	Zog Nit Kénmol **L**
Durme Durme **U**	Mizmor L'David II **H**	
Echad Mi Yodéa **F**	Momele **E**	
El Ginat Egoz **X**	Nolad'ti L'shalom **A**	
Ele Chamda Libi **T**	O'se Shalom **A**	
Eli Eli **V**	Ocho Kandelikas **U**	
Emese Eshes Chayil **W**	Od Lo Ahavti Dai **C**	
	Od Yishama **S**	

ALPHABETICAL INDEX

A Brivele Der Mamen/ 96
A Yidishe Mame /85
Adir Hu /208
Adon Olam /176
Adon Olam II /178
Al Kol Ele /48
Alef Bet /170
Am Yisraél Chai /10
Am Yisraél Chai II /10
Amen Shém Nora /151
Ani Ma'amin /239
Ani Purim /198
Artsa Alinu /22
Avadim Hayinu /203
Avinu Malkénu /219
Az Yashir Moshe /149
B'arvot Hanegev /14
Bai Mir Bistu Shén /81
Bashana Haba'a /32
Belz /98
Bilvavi /213
Birkat Hamazon /236
Candle Blessings /189
Chad Gadya /206
Chad Gadya II /207
Chag Purim /199
Chai /60
Chanuka Chag Yafe /195
Chiribim /112
Chorshat Ha'ekaliptus /12
Chosn Kale Mazel Tov /115
Cuando El Rey Nimrod /122
D'ror Yikra /143
D'ror Yikra II /144
David Melech Yisraél /11
Dayénu /204
Der Rebe Elimelech /76
Di Grine Kuzine /92
Di M'zinke /114
Dodi Li /19
Dona, Dona /162
Durme Durme /128
Echad Mi Yodé'a /209

El Ginat Egoz /46
Ele Chamda Libi /218
Eli Ata /240
Eli Eli /78
Eliyahu Hanavi /187
Erets Yisrél Yafa /20
Erev Ba /23
Erev Shel Shoshanim /37
Esa Enai /216
Eshes Chayil /84
Eshet Chayil 181
Ets Chayim Hi /228
Ets Harimon /139
Ha Lachma Anya /200
Hafinjan /36
Hakotel /44
Hal'luya /58
Halicha L'késaria /31
Hamavdil /153
Hamilchama Ha'achrona /52
Hatikva /68
Hava Nagila /34
Hévénu Shalom Aléchem /11
Hine Ba /194
Hiné Ma Tov /24
Hiné Ma Tov II /25
Hitragut /129
I Have A Little Dreydl /196
Jerusalem Is Mine /160
Jerusalem of Gold /56
K'var Acharé Chatsot /27
Kadésh Ur'chats /146
Kadésh Ur'chats II /147
Ki Eshm'ra Shabat /141
Ki Mitsiyon /227
Kol Ha'olam Kulo /220
L'cha Dodi /174
L'cha Dodi II /175
L'chi Lach /164
L'shana Haba'a /210
L'shana Haba'a II /210
Lach Y'rushalayim /54
Lanér V'livsamim /133

Leaving Mother Russia /158
Light One Candle /167
Lo Yisa Goi /70
Los Bilbilicos /123
Lu Y'hi /16
M'chuténiste Maine /93
Ma Avaréch /47
Ma Nishtana /201
Ma Nishtana II /202
Ma'oz Tsur /145
Ma'oz Tsur /190
Machar /50
Mashiach /242
Mi Y'malél /191
Mipi El /152
Mitsva G'dola /238
Mizmor L'david /134
Mizmor L'david II /136
Momele /156
Moshe Emet /217
My Zédi /168
Nigun /246
Nigun II /247
Nigun III /248
Nigun IV /248
Nolad'ti L'shalom /62
Non Komo Muestro /150
Nye Zu Ritse Chloptsi /244
Ocho Kandelikas /132
Od Lo Ahavti Dai /30
Od Yishama /232
Od Yishama II /233
Oifn Pripitchik /72
Ole, Ole /35
Ose Shalom /19
Papirossen /88
Quen Supiese /148
Rad Halaila /42
Rézele /100
Rozhinkes Mit Mandeln /74
Rumania, Rumania/ 118
S'brent /106
S'vivon /192
Samchém /241
Scalerica D'oro /124
Shabat Hamalka /172

Shabat Shalom /179
Shalom Alechem 180
Shalom Rav /222
Shehecheyanu /234
Shén Vi Di L'vone /102
Sheyibane Bet Hamikdash /225
Shir Hama'alot /185
Shir Hama'alot II /186
Shir Hapalmach /28
Shiro Shel Aba /26
Shloimele Malkele /108
Shmelkie's Nigun /245
Siman Tov /231
Sisu Et Y'rushalayim /66
Sisu V'simchu /188
T'fila /38
Ta'am Haman /130
Tsena 41
Tsiyon /214
Tsur Mishelo /184
Tu Bishvat /197
Tumbalalaika /94
Ufaratsta /224
Un Az Der Rebe Zingt /80
Ush'avtem Mayim/ 18
Uva'u Ha'ovdim /230
V'haér Enénu /221
V'hi She'amda 205
Vi Ahin Zol Ich Gén
Y'did Nefesh /173
Y'mé Hachanuka /193
Y'rushalayim /64
Y'varech'cha /212
Ya Ribon /183
Yankele /90
Yigdal /142
Yism'chu Hashamayim /226
Yitsmach Shalom /138
Yo M'enamori D'un Aire /126
Yom Ze L'yisraél /140
Yome Yome /101
Yossel, Yossel /116
Zara /215
Zemer Atik /40
Zog Nit Kénmol /107
Zol Shoin Kumen Di G'ulo /110

255